Reflexology for Holistic Therapists

Francesca Gould

LEARNING RESOURCES
CENTRE
Havering College
of Further and Higher Education

T

Published in 2005 by:
Nelson Thornes Ltd
Delta Place
27 Bath Road
CHELTENHAM
GL53 7TH
United Kingdom

05 06 07 08 09 / 10 9 8 7 6 5 4 3 2 1

A catalogue record for this book is available from the British Library

ISBN 0 7487 9411 5

Illustrations by Oxford Designers and Illustrators
Page make-up by Pantek Arts Ltd, Maidstone, Kent

Printed in Croatia by Zrinski

Contents

Introduction

Reflexology is a complementary therapy, which involves working on the feet or hands to enable the body to heal itself. It treats the whole person, not just the symptoms of disease, and has proved to be effective for many conditions.

Each year almost 1.5 million people will visit a reflexologist. Businesses are recognising the need for employees to de-stress so are increasingly using reflexology to help cope with the effects of stress. The NHS is also employing reflexologists to work in hospitals. Practitioners can work in clinics, sports centres, beauty salons, hotels, care homes and on cruise liners.

This book is mainly written for the reflexology student studying professional courses such as Association of Reflexologists, VTCT and ITEC reflexology qualifications. It is also a useful reference book for qualified reflexologists.

There is a full reflexology routine and also a section that discusses hand reflexology. This book is designed to be a workbook and there are tasks and activities such as labelling and colouring throughout to aid learning. The multiple-choice section will help you prepare for examinations.

Francesca Gould

April 2005

Dedication and Acknowledgements

DEDICATION

This book is dedicated to my beautiful daughter Charlotte.

ACKNOWLEDGEMENTS

The author would like to thank the model, Andrew Bedale, for the use of his feet and hands for the photographs. Also Heather Mole and Liz Mogridge for reviewing this book.

The author and publishers would like to thank the following for the use of copyright material:

- Dwight C. Byers, President, International Institute of Reflexology copyright 2001 ©, IIR (UK), 146 Upperthorpe, Walkley, Sheffield, S6 3NF www.reflexology-uk.net for the IIR foot chart on page 6.
- Kristine Walker for the hand charts on page 124.
- The Reflexology Academy of Southern Africa for the foot chart by Chris Stormer on page 7.

Introduction to reflexology 1

HISTORY OF REFLEXOLOGY

Ancient history indicates that reflexology was originally practised in Egypt, India and China. Around 2330 BC the tomb of Ankhmahor was built in Egypt and a wall painting, thought to show men practising reflexology on feet, can still be seen in the pyramid. The tomb belonged to an Egyptian physician who was second only to the king. The inscription is thought to read, 'Don't hurt me', and the practitioner replies, 'I shall act so you praise me'. Foot treatment was also widely practised in India and China, and North American Indians traditionally gave foot massage.

Figure 1.1 *Egyptian hieroglyph from the tomb of Ankhmahor*

In China treatment involved using reflexology and acupuncture. Reflexology was used to find energy imbalances or problems and then needles were applied on specific points of the body. In China, around AD 1017,

Dr Wang Wei made a bronze figure that showed the main acupuncture points on the body.

In 1582 Dr Adamus and Dr A'tatis wrote a book about zone therapy, which shows that a type of reflex technique was being practised, particularly in central Europe. Reflexology developed in the late 1800s.

The scientific basis for reflexology comes from neurological studies that were carried out in the 1890s in London by Sir Henry Head. In 1898 he discovered zones on the skin that linked with parts of the spine and internal organs. He stated that 'the bladder can be excited to action by stimulating the sole of the foot'.

In 1902 a German man called Dr Alfons Cornelius wrote the manuscript 'Pressure points, the origin and significance', and was possibly the first to apply massage to reflex zones. He found that if the practitioner spent additional time on areas where the patient suffered discomfort, the pain disappeared and there was an improvement in health.

In the UK, Sir Charles Sherrington (1859–1952) was an Oxford physiologist. He showed that the brain and its nerves could transmit signals around the body to control the body's functions. In 1906 he wrote a book called *The Integrative Action of the Nervous System*.

An American, Dr William Fitzgerald (1872–1942) discovered that the body is made up of zones and developed zone therapy (see Chapter 3). He was an ear, nose and throat surgeon and discovered that pressure applied to various parts of the body (including certain points on the toes and hands) deadened pain in other areas. He was able to carry out minor surgery using this technique.

Fitzgerald and his colleague Edwin Bowers tried to convince others of the effectiveness of the therapy. In 1915 Bowers wrote an article describing the effects of zone therapy entitled 'Stop the Toothache Squeeze Your Toe'. In 1917 Fitzgerald and Bowers published a book called *Zone Therapy*. An American doctor called Joe Riley became very interested in this therapy and studied under Fitzgerald.

Between 1920 and 1930 Joe Riley and his wife Elizabeth developed 'hook work' which involved using the fingers to hook under bones, e.g. the scapula, and this was carried out in connection with zone therapy. Riley created the first diagrams that located reflex points on the foot and ear. The use of the reflex points of the ear is known as auricular therapy (see Chapter 6). He divided the foot into eight horizontal zones. The Rileys had a school that taught zone therapy and in 1919 they published a book called *Zone Therapy Simplified*.

Dr Riley had an assistant called Eunice Ingham (1889–1974), an American physiotherapist. She was the founder of reflexology as we know it today. She discovered that by using a pressure technique across the soles of the feet she was able to stimulate and heal other parts of the body, and she made a detailed chart of the reflexes on the feet.

In 1938 Eunice Ingham wrote *Stories the Feet Can Tell*, and in 1963 she wrote *Stories the Feet Have Told*.

Her nephew, Dwight Byers, continued her work and in 1966 a pupil of hers, Doreen Bayly, introduced reflexology to the UK and opened up a training school.

In the 1960s Robert St. John developed the metamorphic technique from his work in reflexology. He worked mainly on the spinal reflex areas of the feet and was interested in the emotional effects of the treatment.

A German nurse and masseuse called Hanne Marquardt studied with Eunice Ingham and brought reflexology to Germany in 1970. Between 1966 and 1974 she developed transverse zones. She trained doctors and nurses and in 1974 she published a book called *Reflex Zone Therapy of the Feet*.

In 1982 the Rwo Shur Health Institute was founded. The Rwo Shur method was developed in Taiwan by a Swiss missionary called Father Joseph Eugster. The Rwo Shur method of reflexology is practised in many parts of Asia including China, Singapore and Taiwan, and it involves using a combination of thumb-sliding and deep-pressure techniques using the knuckles and sometimes small sticks.

In 1985 Denmark-born Inge Dougans formed the South African Reflexology Society. She showed that the zones of reflexology are linked to the meridians of acupuncture.

Task 1.1

Table 1.1

Name/country	Brief description
Egypt	
China	
Sir Henry Head	
Dr Alfons Cornelius	
Charles Sherrington	
Dr William Fitzgerald	
Dr Joe Riley	
Eunice Ingham	
Doreen Bayly	
Robert St. John	
Hanne Marquardt	
Father Joseph Eugster	
Inge Dougans	

Research the history of reflexology and complete the table above.

WHAT IS REFLEXOLOGY?

Reflexology is a therapy which involves using the thumb and fingers to apply pressure to the feet and/or hands. There are points on the hands and feet that relate to organs, glands and systems of the body. These points are known as reflex points; a reflex is when stimulation at one point brings about a response in another area.

The feet can be thought of as mirroring the body and so the organs and glands etc. can be mapped onto the feet. The left foot mirrors the left side of the body and the right foot reflects the right side of the body. Reflexology charts and diagrams are useful as they show the parts of the feet that relate to the organs etc. The position of reflex points may vary depending on which chart you are using. The charts are only guides and with practice you will instinctively know the area of the feet that relates to the organs etc.

Reflexology is a holistic healing technique, which means the individual's mind, body and spirit are taken into account when giving treatment. That is why a thorough consultation is given. Reflexologists treat the whole body; they do not generally work on one specific organ or system. They treat the symptoms and also aim to treat the cause. They aim to restore balance and harmony to the whole body.

> **Note**
>
> Holistic is a term derived from the Greek word 'holos', which means 'whole'.

The reflexologist

A reflexologist will be compassionate and caring and will want to help restore an individual to good health, but the client must make the decision to get well and be willing to let go of disease. People must understand that there is no such thing as an instant cure; healing is a process. Many diseases take a long time to occur, so it may take a while for the symptoms to be relieved. The reflexologist does not heal, the body heals itself. Be aware that some people may be reluctant to be healed of their illness. Perhaps they receive a lot of attention and sympathy from others due to their problem and are unwilling to give up this attention.

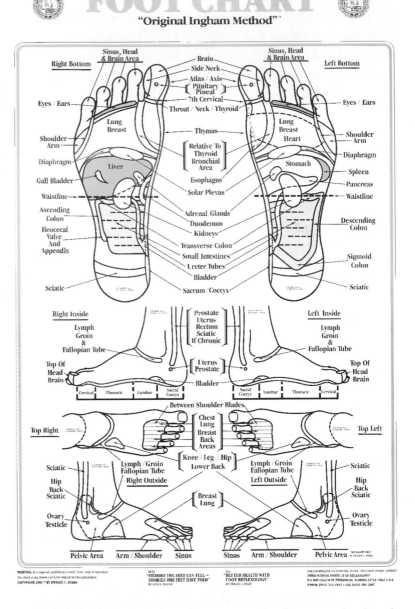

Figure 1.2a *The IIR foot chart: map of reflexes on the feet, by Eunice Ingham*

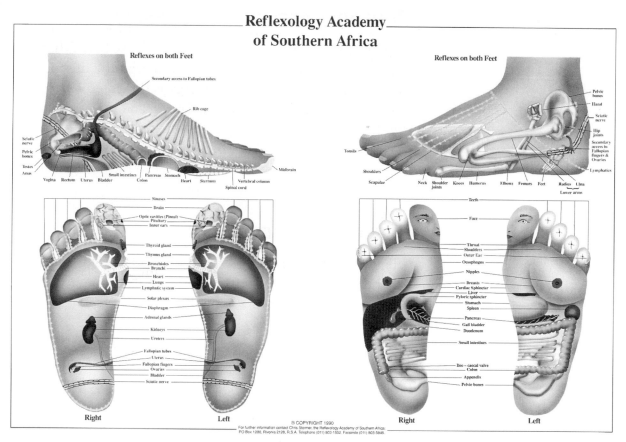

Figure 1.2b *Map of reflexes devised by Chris Stormer*

Reproduced by kind permission of the Reflexology Academy of Southern Africa

Who can benefit?

The elderly, women, pregnant women, men and children can all benefit from reflexology. Babies and children respond well to treatment as they are naturally relaxed and their bodies are very responsive.

Reflexology has proved itself to be effective, but because everyone is individual, what may be of great benefit for one person may not have the same results for another. Reflexology treatment benefits the receiver on several levels – physical, mental and spiritual.

HOW DOES REFLEXOLOGY WORK?

Reflexology is based on the ancient Chinese belief that energy flows around the body. This energy, the life force, is known as Chi and when the energy is flowing freely around the body we are well, balanced and in harmony with our environment physically, mentally and emotionally. If this energy becomes blocked illness may result; unblocking this energy will mean the energy can flow freely so healing can take place.

REFLEXOLOGY THEORIES

There are different theories about how reflexology works and they all agree that reflexology stimulates the body's own healing powers in a natural and safe way.

Wherever there is imbalance or illness in the body, the corresponding area in the foot may be tender or painful. Crystal deposits may be found in the hands and feet. Crystals that are stuck to the end of capillaries and nerve endings are the result of the cells not functioning as well as they should. Working over these areas with the thumbs and fingers will help to break down and get rid of the toxic waste products that have built up and caused the cells to malfunction. Therefore the energy flow is restored.

The crystals are thought to be calcium deposits or uric acid crystals that have settled under the skin surface at the capillary and nerve endings. The circulation of blood can be affected by the build up of these deposits and there may be a decreased flow of blood and lymph in certain areas. Many of these deposits may be found in the feet due to the fact that there are several thousand nerve endings there and because shoes restrict the natural movement of the foot. Gravity may also play a part as it is harder for the blood to flow in an upward direction, so it will tend to stagnate, together with the toxins in the blood, thus causing crystals to form.

Another theory is that when messages are sent along nerve pathways from the brain and/or spinal cord, a tiny amount of waste is produced. This waste consists of lactic acid, uric acid, calcium and various other substances. When a muscle or organ is overstressed, as during illness or at times of extreme stress, these waste products build up and block the flow of energy and the circulation.

During a reflexology session these crystal deposits and waste products can be broken up by applying pressure with the hands and can therefore increase the blood circulation to the area involved. The additional blood and oxygen that is sent to the area of the body corresponding to that reflex point on the foot helps to relax muscles and to flush toxins from organs.

Another explanation of how reflexology works is the meridian theory. Meridians are invisible channels that run through the body carrying energy. The energy can become blocked and reflexology and other therapies, such as acupuncture and shiatsu, can help to release this energy. Acupuncture uses needles to stimulate the energy; shiatsu and acupressure involve applying pressure with the hands. In both cases the blockages are cleared and the body's natural flow of energy is restored.

It is important that both the client and reflexologist have faith in the treatment. The belief that positive results will be achieved is known as the placebo effect. Reflexology treats the mind and spirit as well as the body. Therefore the person's positive state of mind and trust in their reflexologist will further help to ensure that the treatment is successful.

Note

Reflexology will not worsen an ailment and will usually improve the condition. However, reflexology should never take the place of conventional medical treatment.

BENEFITS AND USES OF REFLEXOLOGY

There are many benefits of receiving a reflexology treatment including the following:

- it helps the receiver to relax
- it cleanses and detoxifies the body as toxins are broken down and released into the system
- it helps promote energy flow in the body
- it helps release endorphins which are the body's mood-lifting and pain-killing hormones that are released from the pituitary gland
- it helps the release of serotonin from the brain, which is a substance that helps to lift the mood and is found in anti-depressant drugs
- muscle tone is improved
- the body is encouraged to heal
- it gives the feeling of well-being
- mental stress is reduced
- blood and lymphatic circulations are improved
- it rebalances the whole system therefore restoring homeostasis
- energy levels may be increased
- it helps to treat many ailments to restore health
- it is preventative healthcare to help protect the body from future illness
- it helps the client to cope with their illness.

Reflexology has been shown to be effective for pain (e.g. back pain), headaches/migraine, infertility, arthritis, sleep disorders, injuries, hormonal imbalances, digestive problems (e.g. irritable bowel syndrome) and stress-related conditions.

Note

The body strives to maintain a constant stable internal environment, which is known as **homeostasis**. For instance, the body's temperature, blood pressure, fluid balance etc. all need to be controlled.

STRESS

Stress is an unavoidable part of modern living; how an individual copes is what makes the difference.

Stressors include job pressure, family problems, lack of money, bereavement and illness. We can often deal with short-term stress effectively by taking time out to relax or taking positive action to deal with the stressor. However, long-term stress may cause health problems.

Worrying and feeling anxious may worsen the stressors. Long-term stress affects the flow of blood as it causes blood vessels to constrict, impairs the circulation and lowers the immune system. It has an effect on the nervous, endocrine and digestion systems. All of this leads to toxins and waste build up in the muscles and joints.

At least 70% of illness is stress related. This includes headaches, migraine, depression, menstrual problems, arthritis and constipation.

Effects of stress

Over a period of time the release of adrenaline into the blood stream without a release of energy will cause essential vitamins and minerals such as vitamins B and C to be used up. These are important for the body's immunity so the body will become susceptible to disease and infection. The release of adrenaline from the adrenal glands will cause the blood pressure to increase, which in turn will trigger a build up of a fatty substance in the walls of blood vessels. When the body is relaxed and balanced then the healing process can work efficiently.

In response to a stressful situation the adrenal glands produce an excess of stress hormones such as cortisol. Cortisol can be a dangerous hormone. Increased levels can affect the function of the thyroid and joints and decrease energy. High amounts of cortisol can cause the breakdown of muscle and bone, eventually leading to the bone-thinning disease osteoporosis. It is a medical fact that flooding the system with any hormone will create disease in the body, such as when the thyroid gland produces too many hormones and affects the metabolism.

Disease can be a direct result of an individual's thoughts and actions as these cause chemical changes to take place. The mind is very powerful and affects every cell in the body. Thus, adopting a positive attitude will help to achieve a healthy body and mind.

The negative effects of emotions, stress and lifestyle can cause imbalance in the body. If one part of the body is not functioning efficiently, the whole body suffers. The individual may complain of aches and pains, tiredness and feeling generally run down due to these negative effects.

Integral biology is the study of the effects that our environment has on our health. For example, pollution may cause tiredness and sickness. Too much caffeine may cause anxiety. Poor diet and food that is not organic may cause tiredness and lack of energy. If the eliminative organs, which include the skin, lungs, kidneys and large intestines, are not eliminating toxins properly it can lead to tiredness, spots on the skin, lack of energy etc. Stress at work can lead to digestive disorders, high blood pressure and possible heart problems.

Symptoms of stress

The symptoms of stress include the following:

◊ difficulty in sleeping
◊ feeling lethargic and tired
◊ crying a lot
◊ rarely laugh or smiling
◊ poor concentration
◊ muscle pains

> **Note**
>
> Eunice Ingham said, 'Why poison the body with poisonous thoughts?'

- short temper
- feeling unable to cope
- drinking alcohol or smoking more
- losing temper often
- loss of interest in sex
- generally pessimistic
- loss of appetite
- eating more
- apathy
- negative thinking.

General adaptation syndrome

Physiologist Hans Seyle used the term 'general adaptation syndrome' (GAS) to describe the body's response to stress. He stated that there are three phases.

1   The alarm reaction. The sympathetic nerves come into action as the body prepares for fight or flight. The increased flow of adrenaline (epinephrine) causes the heart to beat faster, the pulse and blood pressure to rise, and breathing becomes quicker and shallower. Other physiological changes also occur when coping with an emergency situation. Symptoms include dizziness, sweating, churning stomach, nausea and poor sleep pattern. The adrenal glands release cortical and other important hormones into the bloodstream at this stage.

2   The resistance stage. The body strives for homeostasis, a state in which blood pressure, heart rate, hormone levels and other vital functions are maintained within a narrow range of normal. The resistance stage happens if stress continues over a long period of time. Blood pressure may remain high and stress-related illnesses might occur. Symptoms include high blood pressure, colds/flu, migraine, insomnia, eczema, depression, anxiety, and excessive smoking and drinking of alcohol.

3 Exhaustion. The body seems unable to make use of cortical hormones that are released from the adrenal cortex in response to stress. Burn-out and exhaustion occurs and major organs become weakened and may function poorly.

Seyle has suggested that chronic stress is harmful to the body due to the side effects of long-term elevated levels of cortical hormones. The immune system does not work as efficiently so the body becomes susceptible to infections, and strain is put on the internal organs.

Reflexology can help reverse the effects of this stress cycle by calming the sympathetic nervous system, causing a reduction in the release of adrenaline. It reduces the symptoms of stress and anxiety, leaving people in a calmer and more relaxed state.

Note

It is thought that 90% of the things we worry about never actually happen.

Advice to stress sufferers

The following advice can be given to someone suffering from negative stress.

- ◆ Do not dwell on past negative events. Free yourself to enjoy what is happening now.
- ◆ Become more assertive, learn to say NO.
- ◆ Turn negative thoughts into positive ones. Negative thoughts never did anyone any good.
- ◆ Worry only about the things you can control, not what you cannot.
- ◆ Become more organised and set regular, attainable goals. Tick them off as you achieve them.
- ◆ Writing things down often helps to clear anxieties and fears from the mind.
- ◆ Take up a hobby or some sort of activity such as yoga or Tai Chi; these are excellent for relaxation.
- ◆ Attend a stress management and relaxation course.
- ◆ Do not be afraid to ask for help, and delegate responsibility to others.

Stress sufferers should be encouraged to reduce caffeine and alcohol intake and also to stop smoking. This will help to limit the amount of toxins being put into the body, which will help the body to deal more effectively with the effects of stress. Diluted fruit or vegetable juices should be drunk in place of tea and coffee. These will supply vitamin C and magnesium. Both are important but easily depleted when a person is stressed.

A healthy well-balanced diet is very important and sufferers should aim to eat a diet high in fruit and vegetables, wholegrain breads and cereals and low in sugar and caffeine to help give them a greater ability to cope with stress. Certain nutrients have been shown to help deal with stress and support the organs that are involved in the stress reaction. Vitamins A, C and E and the minerals zinc and selenium are particularly recommended.

The vitamin B group is largely responsible for the smooth running of the nervous system. A person depleted of vitamins B, C and zinc is also at increased risk of getting many minor infections such as colds, coughs, cold sores etc.

Regular exercise such as walking, yoga and swimming should be recommended. Exercise is a natural way to increase the release of endorphins (opiate-like substances that help to relieve pain and lift the mood).

HEALTHY BREATHING AND BREATHING EXERCISES

People use two types of breathing patterns. Upper-chest breathing lifts the chest upward and outward and the breathing tends to be shallow and rapid, such as during vigorous exercise. Relaxed or diaphragmatic breathing is deeper and slower. As the lower portions of the lungs are filled with air they push down on the diaphragm and cause the abdomen to protrude. For most people, normal, everyday breathing tends to be mostly shallow and rapid.

Breathing is a powerful way to energise and relax the body. When done correctly it requires a person to inhale slowly and deeply through the nose and exhale through the mouth; this prevents the throat from becoming dry.

Slow, deep and rhythmic breathing triggers a relaxation response in the body. Some of these changes include a slower heart rate, muscular relaxation and a feeling of calmness. Relaxation exercises will also trigger a relaxation response in the body.

Breathing exercise

1   Stand with back straight and feet slightly apart. Inhale slowly and deeply through the nose for about four seconds; think about bringing the breath into the abdomen. At the same time raise the arms backward over the head.

2   Momentarily hold the breath and then allow the arms and trunk to fall forwards. (Ensure knees are bent to prevent any strain.) At the same time, breathe out creating a 'Ha' sound.

3   Breathe in slowly and deeply and slowly raise the body back into the standing position. Repeat the exercise twice.

MEDITATION

Meditation has been part of many eastern religions and philosophies. It involves calming the mind and can encourage deep and clear thought and so aid concentration. It helps to relax tense muscles, to lower blood pressure and regulate the breathing rate. Ensure the body is relaxed, warm and comfortable.

There are different ways to meditate and these can involve concentrating on either a candle flame, a mark on the wall, the breathing pattern, or words such as 'relax' or 'calm'.

If for instance you choose to concentrate on the word 'calm', try to focus on this word only. Although thoughts may pass through your head, acknowledge them and let them go, and continue to concentrate on the word 'calm'. Be aware of your breathing; ensure it is deep and slow.

During meditation a mantra, meaning speech, can help to focus the mind. The sound 'om' is often used and can be repeated with every exhalation.

Task 1.2

Practise meditating for about 10 minutes every day.

Meditative breathing exercise

The following simple meditative breathing exercise will help to promote calm breathing.

1 Sit comfortably with your eyes closed. Concentrate on producing a long, deep, smooth exhalation as you breathe out. You will naturally inhale. Allow your breathing to settle into a smooth, regular rhythm.

2 Relax your muscles. Visualise your thoughts as many bubbles and imagine all the bubbles floating away. You feel warm and relaxed.

3 Try to remain focused on your breathing. If other thoughts appear, acknowledge them and then let them float away in bubbles, and again concentrate on your breathing.

4 Practise this exercise for about 10 minutes every day.

RELAXATION EXERCISES

Relaxation exercises can be given to someone who is feeling stressed or anxious.

1 Either sit or lie down and ensure you are comfortable. Breathing slowly and deeply, take in a deep breath as you carry out each hold-and-release exercise. Focus your attention on your feet; let your heels sink into the floor, floating, relaxing. Feel the tension running out of them. Clench the muscles of the lower legs, hold for about five seconds and then relax. They feel heavy and relaxed. Clench the muscles of the upper legs for about five seconds and then relax. Let the feeling of relaxation move up through the legs and flow through the hips and lower back, relaxing more with each breath. Clench the muscles of your buttocks and then relax them. Let your buttocks and pelvis sink into the floor. You feel very relaxed and comfortable. Clench the muscles of your back and then relax them. Picture the muscles of the back becoming longer and wider. The body is feeling heavy and relaxed.

Let your shoulders relax. Tense the muscles of the chest and abdomen and then relax. Feelings of warmth and relaxation are running up through the body. Now tense the muscles in your arms, hold and release. They feel relaxed and floppy. Clench both hands into fist shapes, hold and release. Feel the tension draining out of the arms and hands. Let that feeling of comfort, warmth and relaxation move up to the face and head. Tense the muscles in the face and scalp, hold and then release. Your head feels heavy and relaxed. You feel very warm and comfortable. Your whole body feels heavy and relaxed. Floating, relaxing.

This exercise can be repeated twice. It is a good technique for releasing tension from muscles and so can help with headaches, aches and pains. It is excellent for relaxing the whole body.

2 Close your eyes and take several deep breaths. Begin releasing tension in the neck by rolling the head slowly from side to side. Allow tension to drain from the head, face and neck like melting wax. Feel the

Note

Affirmations may be used during the relaxation exercises such as, 'I feel relaxed' or, 'I feel in control of my life' etc.

tension flowing out of the chest and abdomen. Feel tension being released from the lower back and then the upper back. Visualise all of the tension being carried down through the arms and out through the hands. Shake the hands to help get rid of this tension.

The whole upper body is now free of tension and feels relaxed. Release tension from the buttocks and legs, continuing to breath slowly. Imagine your legs are heavy and relaxed, let your heels sink into the floor. Visualise the flow of tension running down the calves. Now, concentrate on your feet and think about how they feel. Imagine the tension and pressure of walking flowing out of the feet.

Now imagine a warm, healing light penetrating the top of your head and flowing around the body, down your arms and legs and out through the hands and feet taking away all tension and troubling thoughts. This warm light is flowing freely around the body, helping to heal and relax the body.

VISUALISATION

While giving reflexology treatment you can visualise healing light being brought from the universe, into your hands and passing through to the client's feet to aid healing. Visualisation is a useful tool to help you and your client to relax and de-stress. Your client can be encouraged to visualise themselves on a beach or in the countryside while undertaking the relaxation and breathing exercises.

To protect you from the client's negative energies you can imagine yourself in a golden cloak, or visualise an egg shape around your body. (See Chapter 5)

THE PROFESSIONAL THERAPIST

The therapist needs to present a professional image and manner when carrying out reflexology treatment. If the first impression is bad it is unlikely the client will return for further treatment.

PREPARING THE TREATMENT ROOM

The therapy room should be clean, tidy and well presented. Ensure everything is at hand and that towels are folded and the trolley is laid out neatly (perhaps with crystals and an attractive bowl for the powder, oil etc.). You may also consider subdued lighting and relaxing music. There needs to be adequate heating because if the client is cold they will not enjoy the reflexology treatment.

Essential oils may be placed in a burner to help the client relax. In the winter months a couple of drops of essential oil can be put onto cotton wool and placed on a warm radiator. Oils that will help to relax and calm a client include lavender, camomile, rose, neroli, sandalwood, frankincense and clary sage. Ensure you obtain the client's permission before using essential oils.

Equipment and materials

The trolley and couch must be set up before the client arrives for treatment.

Below is a checklist to help you prepare. Ensure you have all of the items listed.

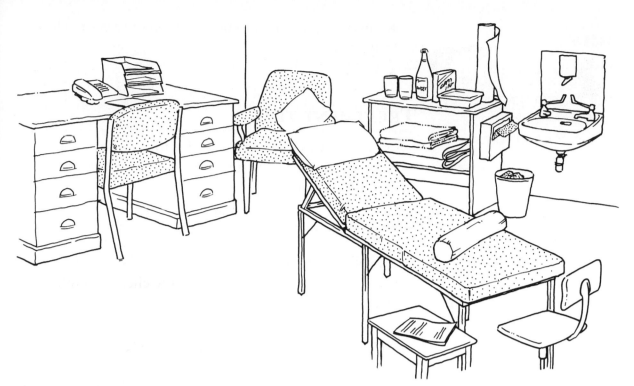

Figure 2.1 *A treatment room furnished with couch and accessories*

Checklist

1   Client consultation form and pen.

2   Large and small clean towels.

3   Couch roll, thin strip of muslin or other hygienic covering.

4   Blanket, in case the client becomes cold.

5   Bolsters and/or rolled-up towels.

6   CD player to play relaxing music.

The trolley should contain the following items:

 ♦ massage mediums; if using cream, disposable spatulas
 ♦ bowls for client's jewellery and for cotton wool

- surgical spirit or antiseptic solution or wipes to clean the feet

- tissues.

TREATMENT TIME

A reflexology treatment will last for three quarters of an hour to an hour. The first treatment may include a lengthy consultation so will take longer.

FREQUENCY OF TREATMENT

You will need to discuss with your client how often the treatment should be carried out. It will depend on their finances, time and their reasons for coming. If they have come for relaxation, they might attend once every two weeks. If they have a particular condition that needs treating, you could suggest attending for treatment once or twice a week for five weeks with a reassessment of the situation after that time. Emphasise to your client the importance of regular treatments to maintain the long-term benefits.

The number of treatments will vary according to the type of condition and the length of time they have been suffering from it. Usually a condition will heal more quickly when it is of recent origin. When the body requires a lot of repair the recovery time will be longer.

CONSULTATION

The consultation is an important part of the reflexology treatment and begins with greeting the client and asking them to sit down. Write the client information on a consultation form. Inform the client that all information given is confidential and that the details will be stored securely. Ensuring client confidentiality will help create a trusting, professional relationship between the client and therapist. You should also look at the client's non-verbal communication, e.g. are they nervous.

The consultation is essential for the following reasons:

- so that you can start to develop a good relationship with the client
- to find out if there are any medical reasons that would prevent the treatment being carried out
- to find out what the client's expectations of the treatment are. If they know what to expect during the treatment, this will also help to reassure a nervous client
- it helps you to treat the client in a holistic way as you can find out about their lifestyle. Emotional factors may be causing persistent aches and pains; maybe their job involves bending their neck a great deal so this is causing neck problems; or perhaps heavy lifting is affecting the shoulders. If the client feels persistently tired, this is often caused by stress and so breathing and relaxation techniques can be taught
- you can discuss the treatment plan, the duration and the cost.

Note

Make a note of points of interest discussed by the client, perhaps an exam, holiday, wedding etc. The next time you meet you can ask how they got on.

Active listening

Active listening means giving the client your full attention when they are speaking. Often we only pay partial attention, we may hear them but we are not listening in a fully receptive way. You must ensure the following when talking with the client:

- make sure you do not switch off and allow your mind to wander
- do not be judgemental
- do not interrupt with your own comments
- do not take over the conversation voicing your own opinions
- do not change the subject.

After the client has spoken, summarise the important points and repeat these back to ensure you have fully understood what they have told you.

Note

During the consultation ensure you ask open-ended questions. Use words such as 'what' and 'how'. You will gain a lot more information from the client.

Below is an example of a reflexology consultation form. The italic text in brackets indicates questions that the therapist should consider asking the client or possible causes/effects of symptoms. Always ensure the client reads the declaration and signs the consultation form.

REFLEXOLOGY CONSULTATION FORM

NAME:	**TEL NO:**
ADDRESS:	
EMAIL ADDRESS:	**D.O.B:**

How did you hear about me?

MEDICAL QUESTIONNAIRE
(Please circle either 'yes' or 'no' and write any relevant details in the space provided)
Are you suffering from or have you suffered from any of the following?

High or low blood pressure	Yes/No
Heart condition	Yes/No
Liver complaints (such as hepatitis, sluggish liver that does not function as well as it could)	Yes/No
Epilepsy	Yes/No
Digestive problems (such as irritable bowel syndrome, diverticulitis, flatulence, discomfort, constipation, diarrhoea)	Yes/No
Are your bowels regular? *(Are they open once each day or less often? Do you suffer from cramps after eating, or piles?)*	Yes/No
Bladder/kidney/urination: do you suffer from cystitis, infections, pain when passing urine?	Yes/No

How would you describe the way that you perspire:

normally	Yes/No
OR	
excessively	Yes/No

(If excessively it could indicate hormonal imbalance)

Do you have thrombosis or an embolism?	Yes/No
Eyes/ears/sense organs: do you suffer from any discomfort, blurred vision, hearing problems etc.?	Yes/No
Do you suffer from headaches? *(Associated with stress, periods, eating or irritable bowel syndrome)*	Yes/No
Respiration/sinuses: do you suffer from asthma, shortness of breath, allergies, frequent colds/flu or bronchitis?	Yes/No
Do you have diabetes? (If so, is it well controlled? Do you suffer from any complication of this condition such as eye problems, lack of skin sensation, poor circulation, skin thinning?)	Yes/No
Menstruation: is it regular, is it painful, are you trying to become pregnant?	Yes/No
Skin disorders: do you have eczema or psoriasis?	Yes/No
Do you have any allergies?	Yes/No
Have you had any accidents/injuries?	Yes/No
Have you had any operations?	Yes/No

Do you have any discomfort/pain in your body? Yes/No
Do you suffer from anxiety/depression? Yes/No
If so, what is the cause?
...
Are you on any medication? Yes/No
Is there any relevant family medical history (e.g. heart/circulatory problems)?

Yes/No
Are you pregnant? Yes/No
Details: *(Expected date of delivery; how client is feeling during pregnancy etc.)*
...
Name of doctor ...
Surgery address ...
Tel no: ...
Is GP referral required? Yes/No
If yes, please sign the following declaration: *(Patient to sign)*
A doctor has been consulted and has no objection to reflexology treatment being carried out.
Signature:_____

LIFESTYLE AND PERSONAL DETAILS
Do you have a partner? Yes/No
Do you have any children? Yes/No
What is your occupation? ...
How do you feel about it? ...
Do you drink alcohol and if so how often? ...
Do you smoke and if so how many each day? ...
Do you take recreational drugs? Yes/No
Do you eat a well-balanced diet? Yes/No
How much fluid do you consume during the day?
...
Do you have around 7–8 hours' sleep each night?
...
How often do you exercise? ...
What are your hobbies, how do you relax? ...
Are you going through any major life changes such as menopause, bereavement, loss of job, retirement etc.?
(Please give details) ...
Would you say your stress levels at home are: high/average/low
Would you say your stress levels at work are: high/average/low
Details if levels are high: ...
Would you say your energy levels are: high/average/poor
Details: ...
Have you had any previous holistic therapy treatments? ...
(Note any observations about the client (e.g. body language that suggests nervousness; condition of skin, nails and hair; posture etc.))
Client declaration
The information I have given regarding my medical details is accurate. I have not knowingly omitted anything that may affect my health or the treatment. I will notify the therapist promptly of any future changes to my health.

Client signature: _____   Date: _____

Figure 2.2 *Reflexology consultation form*

Consent

When treating a child, a person receiving palliative or social care, or someone with learning difficulties, prior to commencing reflexology treatment ensure consent is given by a parent or carer.

PREPARING A TREATMENT PLAN

A treatment plan will ensure you have a plan of action to enable you and your client reach your objectives. The plan will include the client's expectations of the treatment therefore helping to ensure client satisfaction.

You can change your treatment plan to suit you and your client at any time. You can also monitor progress to see if changes are needed.

Reflexology treatment plan

Questions the therapist can ask the client:
What conditions would you like help with today? ...
(E.g. headaches)

What are the symptoms? ...
(E.g. pain over right eye and sometimes nausea)

Which part of body affected? ...
(E.g. right side of head)

How often do you suffer with this/these conditions? ...
(E.g. headaches – twice each week; nausea – twice each month)

How long have you suffered with this/these conditions? ...
(E.g. two years)

What makes it better or worse? ...
(E.g. stress makes it worse; warmth makes it better)

How do you cope? ...
(E.g. I take pain relief tablets and rest as much as possible)

Client's expectations of treatment:
What do you hope to gain from this treatment? ...

Which reflex areas will I pay particular attention to? ...
(E.g. I will ensure I pay particular attention to the endocrine glands and spine)

How often should my client return for treatment? ...
(Client may need to come for regular treatment for a longer period of time if they have suffered a condition for a long time)

Negotiated goals for treatment ...
(What you both hope to achieve after treatment or course of treatment)

Client's role in achieving these goals ...
(How the client will take responsibility to help achieve these goals, e.g. ensure aftercare plan is carried out)

Any special needs? ...
(Client may need extra blanket, help onto couch etc.)

Planned date for review of progress ...
(Both of you can agree a review date)

Notes:

Figure 2.3 *Reflexology treatment plan*

Note

Ensure you also send a leaflet, which briefly explains the treatment, as the doctor may not know what a reflexology treatment entails.

Referral letter to client's doctor

If a client has a contraindication they should obtain advice from their doctor regarding their medical condition and suitability for treatment. A standard letter can be given to their doctor or posted enclosing a stamped addressed envelope. The doctor needs to complete and sign the bottom of the letter to advise their patient if they think there is a medical reason why treatment should not go ahead.

Ideally agreement from their doctor should be obtained in writing. If this is not forthcoming the client should only be treated after signing a written agreement to treatment stating that they have been requested to consult their doctor. Insurance companies often want the client to sign a statement that a doctor has been consulted and has no objection to the patient receiving treatment. This will help to protect both the reflexologist and the client. Disclaimers are not full legal protection but they help. It is wise to consult your insurance company on this matter.

Note

Doctors often do not know what a reflexology treatment entails and therefore cannot give permission for treatment to go ahead; they can only advise their patient. Doctors' insurance does not cover them to give permission or consent for holistic therapy treatments.

CONTRAINDICATIONS AND CAUTIONS

There are contraindications and cautions to reflexology treatments, although many leading reflexologists do not believe that there are any set contraindications. They consider that reflexology can successfully treat or help treatment of most or all diseases and disorders, and that the state of the whole person has to be taken into account when deciding to treat someone with a specific disease. However, it is always wise to err on the side of caution.

```
Address of treatment room

Telephone number

Date

Addressee name and address


Dear Dr (name)
Your patient, (name) of (his/her address) has informed me that he/she is suffering
from (high blood pressure, diabetes etc.).
Please advise me if in your view there is any reason why your patient should not
have reflexology treatment.
Thank you.
Yours sincerely


(Your signature)
(Your name printed)


Dr's advice:


I feel (name of client) would/would not be suitable for reflexology treatment.


Dr's signature ............................... Date ........................
```

Figure 2.4 *Sample letter to a patient's doctor*

Contraindications and cautions to reflexology treatment
include the following:

Note

'Contra' is a Latin word
meaning 'against'.
Indication refers to the
treatment.

- Thrombosis/deep-vein thrombosis (aka DVT):
  reflexology treatment stimulates the circulatory
  system. Thrombosis can be dangerous if the clot
  moves to the brain, lungs or heart.

- Phlebitis: this condition involves inflammation of the veins near to the surface of the body. There is redness, swelling and discomfort in the affected area. This condition can lead to deep-vein thrombosis.

- Varicose veins: pressure should not be applied to varicose veins as it may worsen the condition. Light pressure can be used around the affected area.

- Heart conditions/heart attack: people who have had a heart attack should not be treated for at least three months after the attack. Always seek the advice of a doctor.

- Haemorrhage/internal bleeding: the treatment stimulates the blood circulation so may worsen this problem.

- High/low blood pressure: reflexology is very balancing therefore helpful for these conditions, but regular monitoring by a doctor is advisable.

- Infectious/contagious conditions: there is a risk to the therapist of cross-infection and treatment may cause discomfort to the client.

- Gangrene of legs or feet: give hand reflexology instead.

- Pregnancy/unstable pregnancy: reflexology is safe to have during pregnancy. Care should be taken until week 16 and with all unstable pregnancies or where there is a history of miscarriage. The advice of the midwife should be sought prior to giving treatment.

- Clients on medication or who are alcohol or drug abusers: caution is required as reflexes may not respond to treatment and long-term drug use could affect the sensitivity of the reflexes. There is also a danger that the body may get rid of important medication as reflexology might speed up the release of toxins (including medication) from the body. However, abusers of alcohol or drugs have been helped by reflexology.

- Client under the influence of alcohol or other non-medical drugs (i.e. recreational drugs): the client will not gain the full benefits of the treatment.

Note

If a client is on heavy medication there is a possibility that improved removal of toxins from the bloodstream may reduce the level of the drug in the body.

- Scar tissue: treatment can be given but the affected area should be avoided. If the scar is small, the area may be worked on after six months. If the scar is due to a major operation it may be worked on after two years.

- Before and after surgery/operations: reflexology can be used with care after surgery and will help the area to heal. It can also help prepare a client for surgery.

- Swollen areas and oedema (fluid retention): care should be taken over inflamed or painful areas. Reflexology can be effective in helping to relieve fluid retention.

- Osteoporosis: the bones will be thin and weak. Ask the client to seek their doctor's advice. Always work lightly on patients over 60 as there is a higher tendency to osteoporosis.

- Psychosis/manic depression/mental instability/paranoia: reflexology is helpful but may cause emotional instability. The client will need professional counselling too.

- Epilepsy: in case the reflexology treatment triggers an epileptic seizure, although this is unlikely. Also be aware that the client could fall off the couch if they suffer a seizure.

- Infections of feet: wear gloves or carry out hand reflexology instead.

- Diabetes: light pressure may be used. Diabetics whose diabetes is poorly controlled may have problems such as poor healing in the feet due to bad circulation. The skin may be extremely thin and break easily. There may be nerve damage which will mean loss of sensation in areas such as the feet. Reflexology treatment may affect insulin levels.

- Undiagnosed pain, especially if acute: refer back to the GP if not resolved after five treatments. The practitioner needs to be very experienced as there could be a serious underlying condition.

- Undiagnosed conditions: whether the patient is receiving medical treatment or not, the doctor's advice should be sought.

Note

An acute condition is short-lived; a chronic condition will be suffered for a long time.

◆ Children and the elderly: light pressure should be used and shorter treatments given.

◆ Cancer: reflexology is helpful for pain control and to improve the quality of life of cancer patients. However, treatment of someone suffering with lymphoma (cancer of the lymphatic system) should be avoided in case reflexology causes the cancer to spread around the body, although there is no evidence to suggest this will occur. You should check with the patient's doctor before giving any treatment.

◆ HIV/AIDS: there would obviously be a problem if the client had any cuts or open wounds. If preferred, the practitioner may wear gloves, although it is difficult to carry out a successful treatment whilst wearing gloves.

◆ Fevers: there will be many toxins in the bloodstream and there could be a risk of spreading the infection around the body.

◆ Swelling/fractures/sprains: treatment would obviously be painful; work the referral area (see Chapter 3) or the hand.

◆ Arthritis of the feet: work on the hands instead.

◆ Cuts/bruises/abrasions: these are called localised contraindications and can be worked around.

◆ Sunburn/painful areas/undiagnosed lumps and bumps: work around the affected areas.

◆ After a large meal: blood is being diverted to the small intestines to help the body digest food. Reflexology treatment will help stimulate the circulation so it is advised to give treatment a couple of hours later.

◆ Medication: if you are concerned about the medication being taken by your client, it may be wise to seek their doctor's advice prior to giving treatment.

If you are ever unsure whether it is safe to give a treatment, ask the client to obtain their doctor's advice.

Task 2.1

_____ _____ _____

_____ _____ _____

_____ _____ _____

_____ _____ _____

_____ _____ _____

_____ _____ _____

_____ _____ _____

_____ _____ _____

_____ _____ _____

_____ _____ _____

_____ _____ _____

How many contraindications to reflexology can you remember?
List them above.

REFLEXOLOGY IN A CARE SETTING

Reflexology and the elderly

Elderly people can benefit immensely from reflexology treatment. The therapist may have to use gentler pressure than during a normal treatment and the treatment time may need to be reduced. Many elderly people lack physical contact so reflexology treatment can help them feel cared for. If the foot cannot be worked, a treatment on the hand can be carried out instead.

Factors that need to be considered when giving treatment include the fact that the elderly client's joints may be stiff, the skin and bones may be thin and the circulation poor. They can suffer with numerous conditions such as respiratory disorders, digestive problems, depression, insomnia, lowered immunity and urinary conditions. Reflexology treatment can help with all of these problems.

Reflexology and people with disabilities or special needs

Conditions such as muscle spasm, digestive disorders, insomnia and lowered immunity may be experienced by people with disabilities or special needs. Providing the client does not have any contraindications to the treatment, reflexology can help with these problems. The treatment time may need to be reduced.

Giving reflexology treatment in hospital

If a patient spends most of their time in bed or cannot move around easily, their circulation may be poor and reflexology can help stimulate the circulation. Reflexology helps to compensate for lack of exercise in cases of illness or old age and will also help the patient to cope better with their illness.

Obviously the therapist will need to know if there are any contraindications to treatment and if the client is taking any medication. This should be noted on the client's form and the doctor can give advice regarding the suitability of the patient receiving treatment.

REFLEXOLOGY AND THE TERMINALLY ILL

People who are terminally ill can benefit enormously from this treatment. It helps to calm and relax a patient, therefore reducing feelings of anxiety. If the person is suffering pain, reflexology can help to reduce it. The physical touch from the therapist can make the patient feel cared for. The doctor's advice will need to be sought prior to giving treatment.

HANDLING REFERRAL DATA FROM PROFESSIONAL SOURCES

If a healthcare professional (be it a doctor or an aromatherapist etc.) should refer a client to you for reflexology treatment, it is courteous to keep them informed of the client's progress. A progress report should include the following information:

- the client's name, who referred them and their reason for coming for reflexology treatment
- the client's progress
- treatment plan for the future.

A brief letter can be written reporting the progress of the client.

As it is important for a reflexologist to work within the realms of their own expertise, you may occasionally want to refer your client to another health professional such as a doctor, nurse, counsellor, complementary therapist or member of the social care team.

Note

Ensure you have the client's permission before sending the progress report.

Salon address
Telephone number

Date
Addressee name and address

Dear Dr Douglas

Thank you for recommending Sara Smith of 1 High Street, Anytown to come for reflexology treatment. I am writing to inform you of her progress.

Sara has been having regular weekly treatments for the past month to help treat her back problem. Sara feels that the treatments have helped ease the muscle stiffness in her back and as a result she is experiencing less discomfort.

We are to continue her treatments for two more weeks and then she will return to me on a monthly basis.

If you require any further information please do not hesitate to contact me.

Yours sincerely

Ms F. Gould

Figure 2.5 *Sample progress letter to a client's doctor*

EVALUATION OF TREATMENT

It is important to evaluate the reflexology treatment given to the client. How could you have improved the treatment? Ask the client questions such as: 'Did you enjoy the treatment?'; 'Did the treatment meet with your expectations?'; 'Did you find the treatment relaxing, and if not, why?'; 'Have you had an improvement in your symptoms?' A feedback form may be given to a client to fill in. It will help establish which aspects of the treatment may need improvement.

ANATOMY AND PHYSIOLOGY OF THE FEET AND HANDS

There are some common terms that are used to describe different areas of the feet and these will help you to understand the anatomy of the feet. Lateral ① relates to the outside of the foot. Medial ② relates to the inside surface of the foot. Dorsal ③ relates to the top of the foot and plantar ④ relates to the bottom of the foot.

Task 3.1

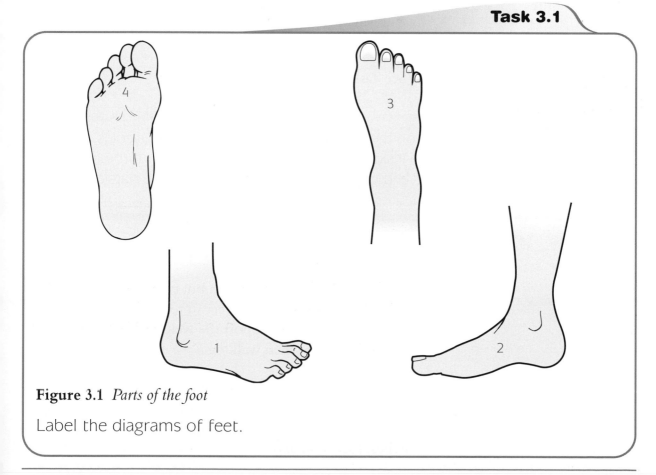

Figure 3.1 *Parts of the foot*

Label the diagrams of feet.

Bones of the lower leg and foot

The lower leg consists of the tibia ① and fibula ②. The bones of the feet make up a bridge-like structure. The foot has 26 bones in total, made up of seven tarsal (ankle) bones, which form the posterior part of the foot and include:

- ◆ one calcaneus ③ (the heel bone). The Achilles tendon is attached to it
- ◆ one talus ④ which is situated above the calcaneus
- ◆ one cuboid ⑤ – the outer side of the foot, in front of the calcaneus
- ◆ one navicular ⑥ found in front of the talus
- ◆ three cuneiform bones ⑦ found in front of the navicular
- ◆ metatarsals ⑧ – there are five metatarsal bones
- ◆ phalanges ⑨ – there are 14 bones that form the toes: two in the big toe and three in the other four toes.

(See Task 3.2)

Note

The bottom end of the tibia on the medial surface is the medial malleolus. It can be felt as a protrusion on the inside of the ankle. The bottom end of the fibula is called the lateral malleolus and can be felt as a protrusion on the outside of the ankle.

Arches of the feet

The foot is not flat underneath but contains curves known as arches. The bones of the feet fit together to form these arches. They help to support the weight of the body and provide leverage when walking.

The arches of the foot are the medial longitudinal arch ①, lateral longitudinal arch ② and transverse arch ③. Strong ligaments and tendons support the bones that form the arches. (See Task 3.3)

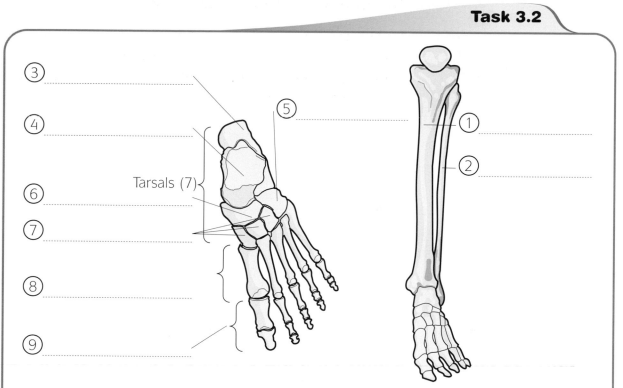

Tarsals (7)

Figure 3.2 *Bones of the lower leg and foot*

Label the foot diagram. Lightly shade the tibia pink, the fibula grey, the calcaneus blue, the talus yellow, the cuboid green, the navicular orange, the cuneiforms purple, the metatarsals brown and the phalanges red.

Muscles and ligaments of the lower leg and foot

The muscles of the lower legs and feet include the gastrocnemius ①, soleus ②, tibialis anterior ③, tibialis posterior ④, peroneus longus ⑤, peroneus brevis ⑥, extensors hallucis longus ⑦, extensor digitorum longus ⑧, flexor hallucis longus ⑨, flexor digitorum brevis ⑩, flexor digitorum longus ⑪, peroneus tertius ⑫, abductor hallucis ⑬ and extensor digitorum brevis ⑭. (See Task 3.4)

Figure 3.3 *Arches of the foot*

Label the diagram.

Arteries, veins and nerves of the leg and foot

The following arteries can be found in the legs and feet: anterior tibial ①, peroneal ②, posterior tibial ③, dorsalis pedis ④, digital ⑤, femoral ⑥, iliac ⑦ and plantar arch ⑧.

The following veins can be found in the legs and feet: saphenous ⑨, femoral ⑩, popliteal ⑪, short saphenous ⑫, and dorsal venous arch ⑬.

The following nerves can be found in the legs and feet: peroneal ⑭, saphenous ⑮, tibial ⑯, sural ⑰ and sciatic ⑱. (See Task 3.5)

Hands, wrist and forearm

Bones

Bones of the forearm and hands include the radius ① (situated on the thumb side of the forearm) and the ulna ② (situated on the little finger side of the forearm). There are eight small bones of the wrist, known as carpals, and these include: the scaphoid ③, trapezium ④, trapezoid ⑤, capitate ⑥, hamate ⑦, pisiform ⑧, triquetral ⑨ and lunate ⑩. (See Task 3.6)

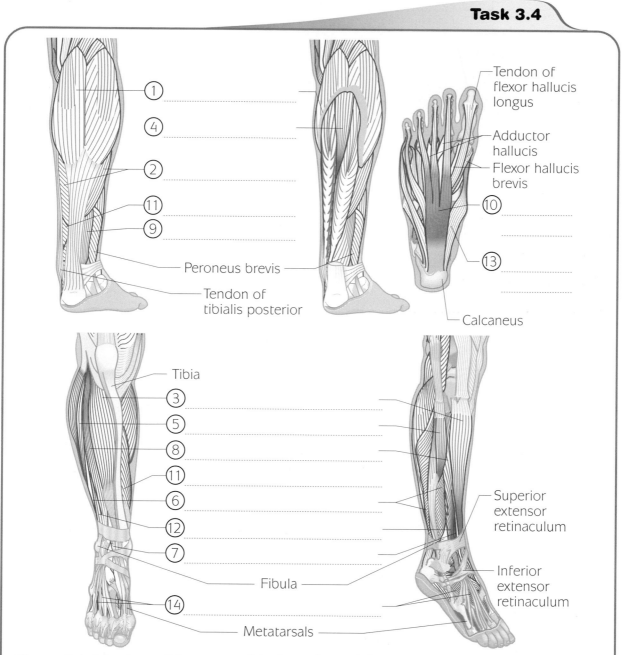

Labels on the diagram:
- ① ④ ② ⑪ ⑨ Peroneus brevis — Tendon of tibialis posterior
- Tendon of flexor hallucis longus
- Adductor hallucis
- Flexor hallucis brevis
- ⑩ ⑬ — Calcaneus
- Tibia — ③ ⑤ ⑧ ⑪ ⑥ ⑫ ⑦ — Fibula
- ⑭ — Metatarsals
- Superior extensor retinaculum
- Inferior extensor retinaculum

Figure 3.4 *Muscles and ligaments of the lower leg and foot*

Label the diagram. Lightly shade the gastrocnemius red; tibialis anterior and tibialis posterior yellow; the soleus blue; the peroneus longus, brevis and tertius green; the extensors orange; the flexors brown; and the abductor hallucis purple.

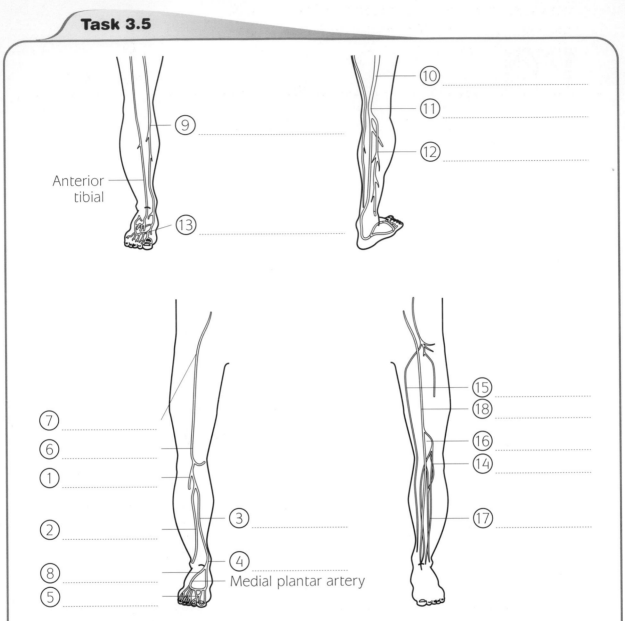

Figure 3.5 *Arteries, veins and nerves of the leg and foot*

Label the diagram. Colour the nerves in yellow, the arteries red and the veins blue.

The metacarpals ⑪ consist of five metacarpal bones which form the palm of the hand. The phalanges ⑫ are the bones of the fingers; there are 14 altogether.

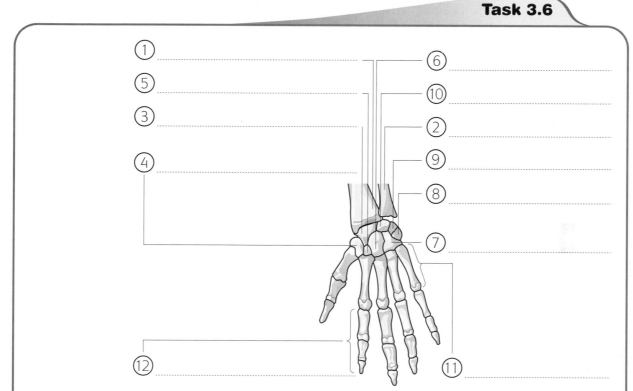

Figure 3.6 *Bones of the lower arm and hand*

Label the diagram. Colour the radius yellow, the ulna red, the lunate, pisiform and trapezoid green, the scaphoid and hamate blue, the triquetral, trapezium and capitate orange. Shade the metacarpals brown and the phalanges purple.

Muscles

Muscles of the forearm, wrist and hand include: the flexor carpi ulnaris ①, flexor carpi radialis ②, pronator teres ③, brachialis ④, extensor carpi ulnaris ⑤, extensor carpi radialis ⑥, extensor digitorum ⑦, extensor pollicis longus ⑧, brachioradialis ⑨, thenar muscles ⑩ (known as thenar eminence) and hypothenar muscles ⑪ (known as hypothenar eminence).

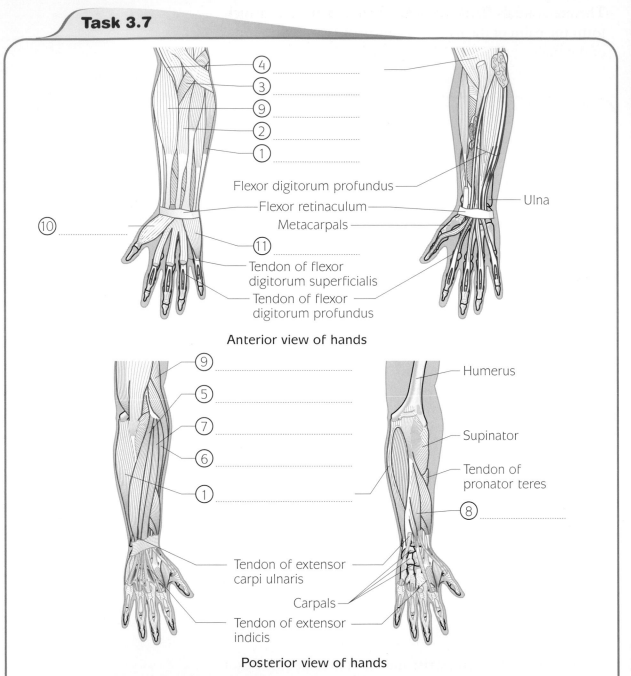

Anterior view of hands

Posterior view of hands

Figure 3.7 *Muscles and ligaments of the forearm and hand*

Label the diagram. Colour the flexors yellow, the extensors orange, the brachialis blue, brachioradialis red, thenar muscles green and hypothenar muscles purple.

Arteries, veins and nerves of the arm and hand

The following arteries can be found in the arm and hand: radial ①, ulnar ②, palmar arches ③ and digital ④.

The following veins can be found in the arm and hand: the median ⑤, cephalic ⑥, basilic ⑦ and axillary ⑧.

The following nerves can be found in the arm and hand: the ulnar ⑨, radial ⑩ and median ⑪.

Task 3.8

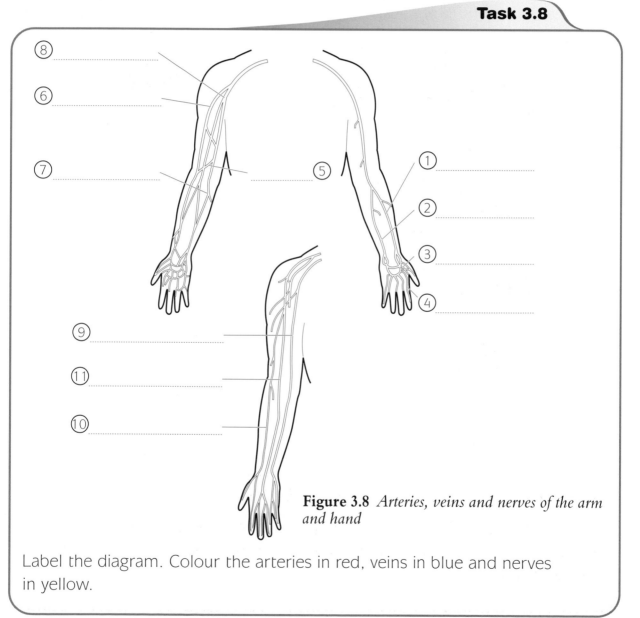

Figure 3.8 *Arteries, veins and nerves of the arm and hand*

Label the diagram. Colour the arteries in red, veins in blue and nerves in yellow.

Table 3.1 Conditions that affect the hands, nails and feet

Condition	Description	Causes
Athlete's foot (tinea pedis)	Many people have the fungus present on their skin, but they are unaffected by it. Breaks in the skin allow the fungus to enter and may cause athlete's foot, which mostly affects the area between the toes and on the sole of the foot. Skin is cracked and itchy with flaking pieces of dead, white skin. Skin may also be swollen and blisters may form. May smell unpleasant	Fungal infection. Highly infectious so the affected area should be avoided during treatment. Anti-fungal powders can be used to treat the condition. If athlete's foot is left untreated it can spread to other parts of the foot, the hands and even the face
Arthritis	Inflammation of one or more joints. Pain and stiffness may also be present in muscles near the joint. (Hallux rigidus is arthritis of the main joint of the big toe which is found in the ball of the foot. It causes stiffness of the big toe)	Osteoarthritis (most common) due to age and wear and tear of joint. Rheumatoid arthritis is an auto-immune condition in which the membrane that lines the joint becomes thick and swollen, and usually affects the fingers and toes
Bunion (hallux valgus)	Displacement of the bone at the base of the big toe occurs. The big toe points towards the smaller toes. The bones, tendons, ligament and sesamoid bones also become displaced and so the joint	Causes include ill-fitting shoes (so the condition is more common in women) and hereditary factors. It may also be due to arthritis, injury or weak ligaments

	at the base of the big toe protrudes. It can be painful, so the foot should be handled gently	
Bursitis	Some joints, including the toes, contain a bursa, which provides padding where tendons rub against bones or other tendons. Bursitis is inflammation of the bursa	Causes include injury to the foot and poorly fitting shoes
Calluses and corns	Areas of hard skin that build up in order to protect areas of the feet from friction or pressure. May be painful. Corns may develop a core, known as a root	Poorly fitting shoes, stretched ligaments in foot and walking barefoot on hard and dry surfaces
Carpal tunnel syndrome	Pain in fingers, hands, forearms, shoulder and/or upper back. Pain can be felt as either a burning pain or shooting pain and there may also be numbness or tingling	Due to compression of the median nerve at the wrist. Causes include repetitive use of hands causing the tendons to swell and fluid retention
Chilblains	Painful itchy areas on the feet, varying in colour from dull blue to red. Mostly affects the elderly and those who work in cold or damp conditions	Poor blood circulation, which is worsened by cold and damp conditions
Diabetes	Feet may be dry, pale and cool to the touch. Poor nerve and blood supply to the muscles and skin results in poor healing of the skin on the feet and there is an increased risk of infection	Due to insufficient production of insulin, or tissues do not respond to insulin. Therefore, there is a build up of glucose (sugar) in the blood

Table 3.1 (continued)

Fallen arches (*pes planus*)	Collapse of one or both arches of the feet. May cause the ankle to lean inward. There is weakness or tearing of ligaments or muscles of the foot	It may be due to excess body weight, ill-fitting shoes, injury and hereditary factors
Gout	A type of arthritis that typically affects the big toe. There may be pain, inflammation and swelling	This condition is due to excessive uric acid in the blood, which forms crystals. Due to too much protein in the diet or hereditary factors
Hammer toes	Deformity of the toes resulting in bent toes. Corns will often develop on the joints of the toes. May be painful	May be due to arthritis, bunion, ill-fitting shoes or hereditary factors
Heel spurs	Due to abnormal growth of the heel bone. Heel spurs can cause extreme pain especially while standing or walking	Excess body weight, prolonged standing or ill-fitting shoes, flat feet or high arches
High arches (*pes cavus*)	Feet have abnormally high arches and may result in a condition known as claw foot	Hereditary factors
Ingrowing toenails	Inflammation due to corner of the nail growing into the skin. Swelling, redness and often painful. Usually affects the big toe	Pressure from footwear and cutting nails too far down. Also hereditary factors, e.g. the nails may be too large
Nail infections (fungal: Tinea ungium)	At first there are white or yellow patches of discolouration. Later the nail becomes thickened, deformed and has a foul odour (musty smell).	Due to fungal infection. Sweaty shoes and moist socks make ideal living conditions for the fungi. May also be due to injury, ingrowing toenail,

	The affected nails may also split and start to crumble	incorrect nail cutting or lowered immunity, e.g. diabetes. Avoid touching the affected areas. Warn the client that it may spread to the other nails
Osteoporosis	Bones are brittle and weak and may break easily	May be due to factors such as ageing, hormonal disorders, hereditary factors and menopause
Plantar fasciitis	Inflammation of a ligament called the plantar fascia that runs from the heel to the ball of the foot. There is pain at the heel or arch when standing	Conditions in which the feet are not aligned correctly, such as fallen arches, can lead to plantar fasciitis. May also be due to injury
Ram's horn (aka club nail)	Over-production of horny cells cause the nail plate to enlarge and this leads to curvature of the nail, similar to a ram's horn	More common in the elderly and the big toe is mostly affected. Causes include age, injury, ill-fitting shoes and neglect. May be associated to a heart and lung condition
Verruca (aka plantar warts)	Raised areas that can be found on the underside of the foot and may contain dark-coloured dots within them. These are small blood vessels. Some disappear by themselves	Due to a viral infection. The affected area should be avoided during treatment. On the hand it is known as a wart and on the foot a verruca

Chapter 7 covers nail infections in more detail.

Note

To help treat a verruca, regularly apply a banana skin to it.

REFLEXOLOGY FOOT CHARTS

There are a variety of foot and hand charts, which can cause confusion for the reflexology student. Different charts may show reflex points in different places. It is important to remember that these charts are only guides, and with lots of practice and experience you will learn the position of the reflexes.

On the following page is an example of a foot chart. The toes represent the head, the widest part of the foot the shoulders, the slimmest part of the foot the waist and the heel is the pelvic area.

ZONE LINES

The feet are divided into 10 zones through which energy passes. This energy connects organs and other parts of the body that lie within the same zone, e.g. the kidneys and the eyes. (See Task 3.10)

Note

All five zones can also be found in the big toe.

- Zone 1 runs through the centre of the body.
- Zone 2 runs through the eye, the body and to the first finger and second toe.
- Zone 3 runs through the eye to the second finger and third toe.
- Zone 4 runs down through the ear and on to the third finger and fourth toe.
- Zone 5 runs from the ear to the little finger and fifth toe.

Locate the following reflex points and shade them red.

- Ovaries
- Pituitary gland
- Gall bladder
- Adrenal gland
- Sciatic nerve
- Breast/chest
- Thoracic spine
- Bladder
- Hip
- Heart
- Ears/eyes
- Fallopian tube
- Solar plexus
- Ascending colon
- Stomach

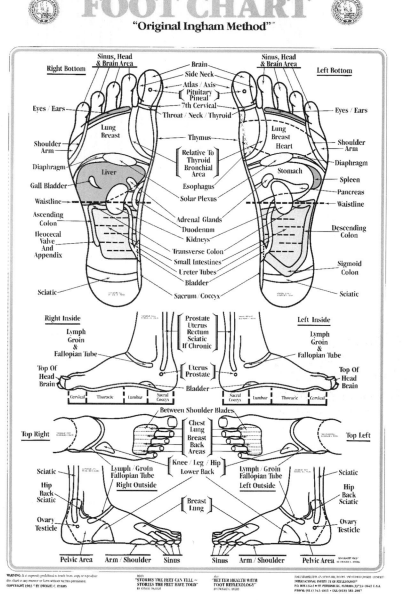

Figure 3.9 *The Ingham foot chart, by Eunice Ingham (Reproduced by kind permission of Dwight C Byers, President, The International Institute of Reflexology)*

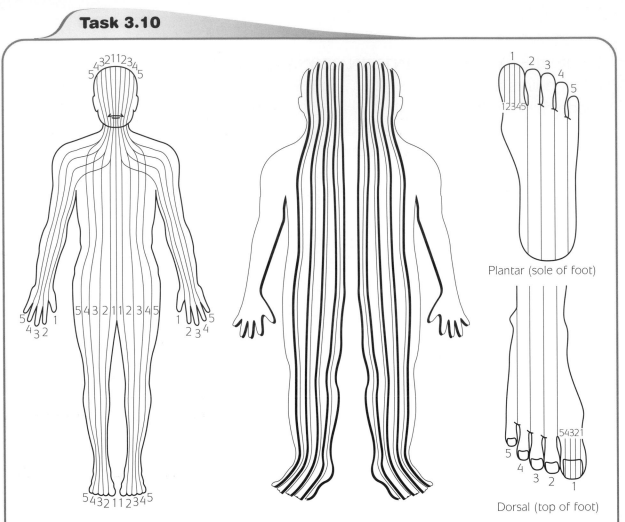

Figure 3.10 *Longitudinal zones of the body and feet*

On the diagram lightly shade zone 1 in red, zone 2 in blue, zone 3 in green, zone 4 in yellow and zone 5 in orange.

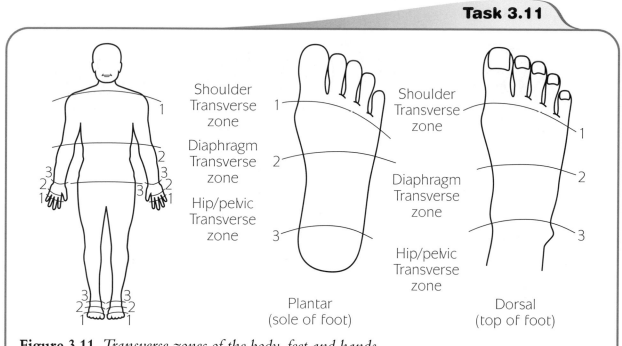

Figure 3.11 *Transverse zones of the body, feet and hands*

Colour the area above the shoulder line in blue, the area above the diaphragm line in red, the area below the diaphragm line in yellow and the area below the hip/pelvic line in green.

TRANSVERSE ZONES

There are also transverse zones in the foot. Dividing the foot this way helps to locate specific reflex points, e.g. the kidneys.

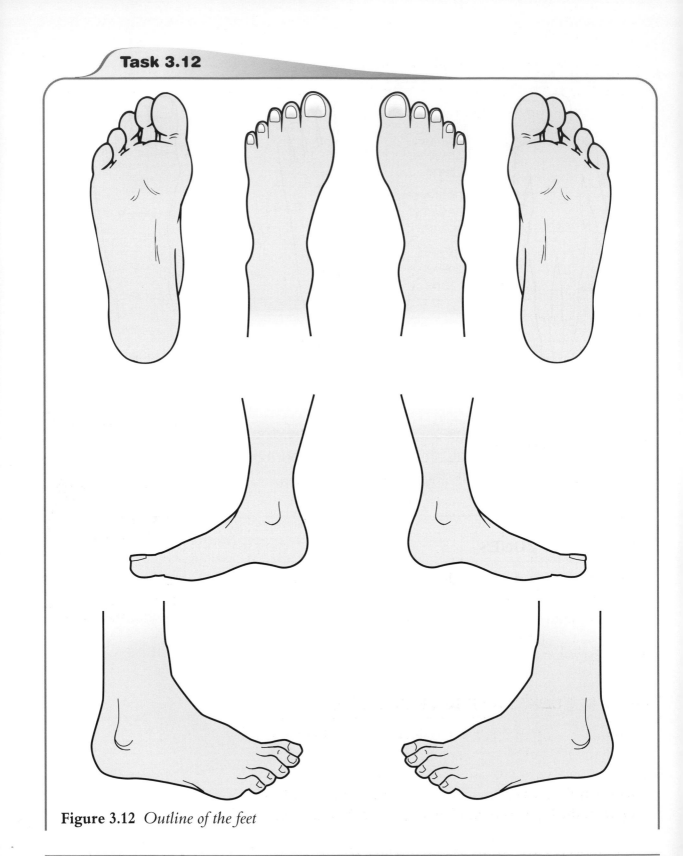

Figure 3.12 *Outline of the feet*

Draw the longitudinal zones and transverse zone onto the foot diagram. Draw and label the following reflexes onto the diagram: (see Chapters 4 and 5 to help complete this task)

- liver
- kidneys
- solar plexus
- large intestine
- spleen
- pancreas
- hypothalamus
- ovary/testicle
- uterus/prostate
- sinuses
- sciatic nerve

- fallopian tubes
- thyroid
- adrenal glands
- ears/eyes
- heart
- stomach
- small intestine
- lungs
- chest/breast
- spine
- hip.

MERIDIAN THEORY

This Chinese theory is that energy flows around the body through channels known as meridians, which unite all parts of the body. Free-flowing energy is essential to ensure harmonious balance in the body and thus good health. Meridians present in the feet pass through all major body organs. Applying pressure to the feet stimulates not only the reflexes and related body parts but also the six main meridians helping to clear congestion and stimulate the circulation of vital energy thus energising the whole body. See Chapter 9 for more information.

Note

Remember that the positions of certain reflexes can vary according to which chart you follow.

CROSS REFLEXES AND REFERRAL AREAS

Areas in the body such as the shoulder and hip, elbow and knee, wrist and ankle, and hand and foot are all related. These are known as cross reflexes or referral areas. For instance, if the area of the foot that represents the shoulder is injured, the hip area of the foot can be worked instead.

Foot = Hand
Sole of foot = Palm of hand
Top of foot = Back of hand
Big toe = Thumb
Small toes = Fingers
Ankle = Wrist
Calf = Forearm (inner)
Shin = Forearm (outer)
Knee = Elbow
Thigh = Upper arm
Hip = Shoulder

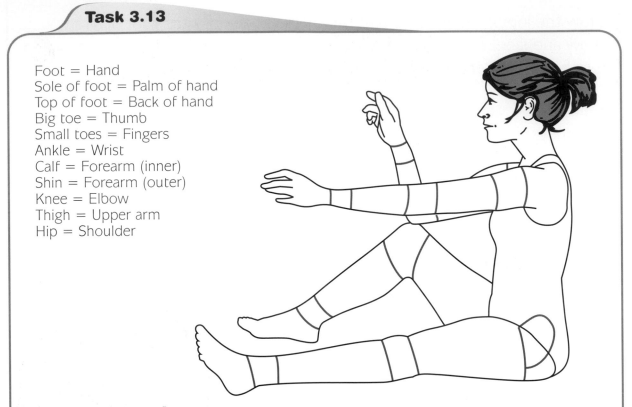

Figure 3.13 *Cross reflex areas*

Use different colours to show corresponding cross reflexes, e.g. red to indicate that the knee corresponds to the elbow.

Understanding reflexology 4

BODY SYSTEMS AND REFLEXOLOGY

The different systems are discussed briefly and particular attention is paid to areas of the body that are worked during the reflexology treatment.

SKELETAL SYSTEM

There are 206 bones in the adult body. Bone is living tissue and is constantly being built up and broken down. It is made up of 30% living tissue and 70% minerals and water. The minerals include mainly calcium and phosphorus.

Vertebral column (spine)

The vertebral column supports the upper body and encloses and protects the spinal cord. It consists of 33 bones, which are divided into five groups known as the cervical, thoracic, lumbar, sacral and coccygeal.

When you are working along the spinal area remember you are working over muscles and nerves too. Therefore, working this area helps conditions involving problems with nerves or muscles.

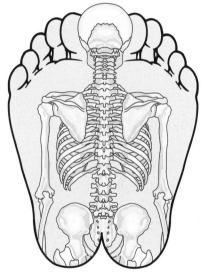

Figure 4.1 *Bones of the body superimposed on the feet*

Note

Regular exercise is essential as it not only prevents loss of bone but also stimulates the formation of new, stronger bone tissue. Bones adapt to the stress of exercise by laying down more calcium and other minerals and also increasing the amount of collagen fibres.

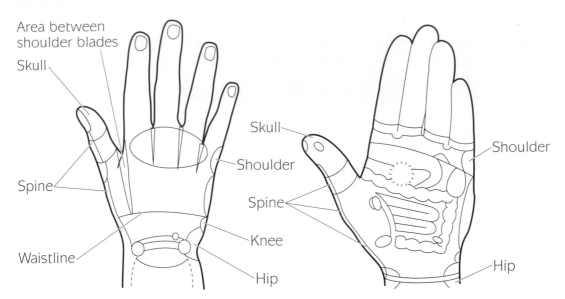

Figure 4.2 *Relevant parts of the hands that relate to the bones of the body*

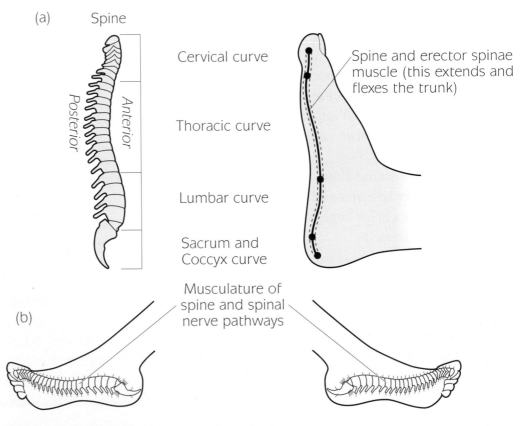

Figure 4.3 *The spine represented on the foot*

Notice that the curves of the spine match the curves of the foot. The shape of the feet often correspond to the shape of the person. For instance a tall, slim person will often have long, slim feet.

Note

The spine supports the weight of the body. If someone is suffering back problems, this may be due to the fact that they feel they are not getting enough support from people at that present time.

Ligaments

Ligaments consist of bands of strong, fibrous connective tissue, which are silvery in appearance. They prevent dislocation by holding the bones together across joints, but stretch slightly to allow movement.

Tendons

Tendons consist of white, strong, almost inelastic, fibrous bands. Most muscles are attached to bones by tendons, which vary in length and thickness. When a muscle contracts, it forces the tendon to move and therefore creates movement at the bone. An example of a tendon is the Achilles tendon that attaches from the calf muscle to the heel.

Note

The cuboid bones in the foot relate to the hip in the body. If these bones protrude it may indicate a weakness in the hip region.

Effects of reflexology on the skeleton and joints

- ◆ A layer of connective tissue called the periosteum covers bones. Blood vessels from the periosteum penetrate the bone, providing the bone with nutrients. Reflexology stimulates blood flow to the periosteum and so increases the supply of nutrients to the bone.

- ◆ Reflexology helps to ease stiff joints and loosen adhesions such as scar tissue in structures around joints. The joints are nourished due to the increased blood supply which brings oxygen and nutrients to the area.

Note

Ligaments and tendons have a poor blood supply so when they are damaged they can take a while to heal.

MUSCULAR SYSTEM

There are over 600 muscles in the body, and these make up 40–50% of the body's weight. The function of the muscles is to produce movement, maintain posture and provide heat for the body.

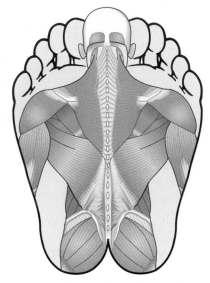

Figure 4.4 *Body and muscles superimposed on the foot*

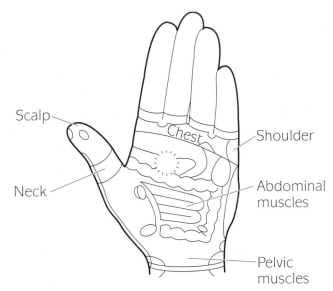

Figure 4.5 *Muscles of the body represented on the hands*

Muscle tone

Muscle is never completely at rest; it is always partially contracted and this is known as muscle tone. The partial contraction is not enough to move the muscle but will cause some tension. All skeletal muscles must be slightly contracted if the body is to remain upright. If the body's muscle tone is good the tone of muscles in the feet will also be good.

Muscle strain

Overwork or overstretching of the muscles can cause strain and may result in muscle fibres being torn. This may be felt as hardness in the corresponding area of the foot.

Tearing of muscle fibres

Injury to a muscle can cause partial tearing of some muscle fibres and the muscle will feel very tender and painful especially when contracted. The corresponding area of the foot may also feel tender.

Cramp

Cramp is a painful muscle spasm that may occur following exercise. Muscle spasms occur when muscles contract for too long, or when excessive sweating causes water and salt loss. The accumulation of lactic acid in the muscles following vigorous exercise may also cause cramp. Light massage and gradual stretching of the affected muscle can relieve the spasm and pain. Sometimes cramp can occur for no reason, such as during sleep, and this may be due to poor muscle tone.

Effects of reflexology on the muscular system

- The blood supply to the muscles will be increased during reflexology, bringing fresh oxygen and nutrients and removing waste products such as lactic acid. This can help to alleviate muscle fatigue.

- Reflexology will help to relieve pain, stiffness and fatigue in muscles as the waste products are removed and normal functioning is quickly restored. The increased oxygen and nutrients will aid tissue repair and recovery of the muscle.

- Reflexology can help the breakdown of fibrositic nodules, also called knots, that develop within a muscle due to tension, injuries or poor posture. Knots are commonly found in the shoulder area of the body and may be felt as granules in the feet.

- It will help to relax muscles that are tense and contracted.

Note

Vigorous exercise can cause minor tearing of muscle fibres and this is thought to be one of the main reasons why muscles become sore and stiff 12 to 48 hours later.

THE CARDIOVASCULAR SYSTEM

The cardiovascular system consists of the heart, blood and blood vessels. The function of the heart is to act as a pump to move the blood around the body. The blood carries oxygen and nutrients and is transported in the body in a series of pipes called blood vessels.

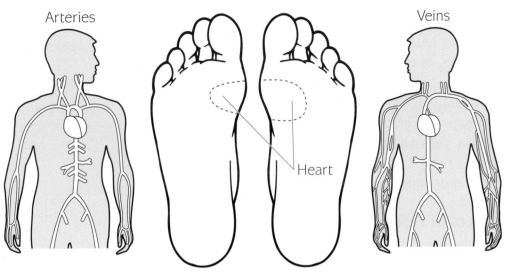

Figure 4.6 *The cardiovascular system (arteries, veins and the heart) and the feet*

> **Note**
>
> There are over 60 miles of blood vessels in the body. The blood circulation in the body will be stimulated when carrying out treatment on the feet.

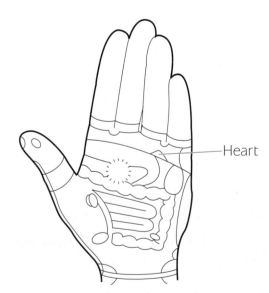

Figure 4.7 *The cardiovascular system and the hands*

Effect of reflexology on the cardiovascular system

- The increased circulation will cause fresh, oxygenated blood and nutrients to be brought to the area and so will nourish the tissues and help with tissue repair. Waste products (metabolic waste) are removed and carried away by the veins. A build-up of waste products can cause pain and stiffness and so reflexology can help to relieve these symptoms.

- Regular reflexology treatments may help to reduce high blood pressure and raise low blood pressure as it helps to rebalance the body.

> **Note**
>
> In Chinese medicine the heart is associated with the emotion of joy, so working this reflex will help people suffering with conditions such as depression.

THE LYMPHATIC SYSTEM

Lymph nodes, lymph, lymph vessels and lymphatic ducts all make up the lymphatic system, which is closely related to blood circulation.

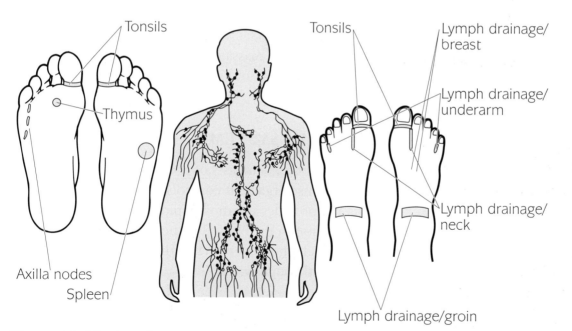

Figure 4.8 *The lymphatic system and the foot*

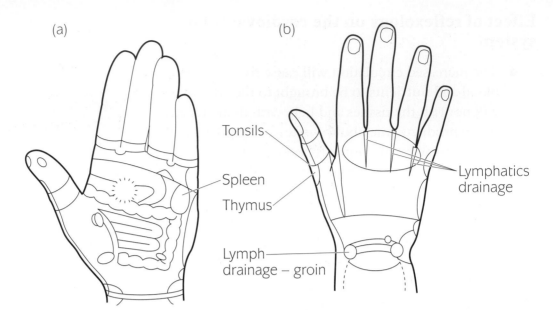

(a)   (b)

Tonsils

Spleen

Thymus

Lymphatics
drainage

Lymph
drainage – groin

Figure 4.9 *The lymphatic system and the hands*

Effects of reflexology on the lymphatic system

◆ It helps to speed up the flow of lymph in lymph vessels therefore helping to detoxify and improve immunity.

◆ Reflexology and massage can help reduce or even prevent oedema (fluid retention) as it improves lymphatic flow.

THE NERVOUS SYSTEM

The nervous system consists of the brain, spinal cord, nerves and sense organs. It controls all of the bodily systems and provides the most rapid means of communication in the body. The nervous system can be likened to a telephone network with messages continually being passed through wires.

Note

In Chinese medicine the spleen is associated with the emotion of worry. It is said that worry and excessive contemplation will damage the spleen.

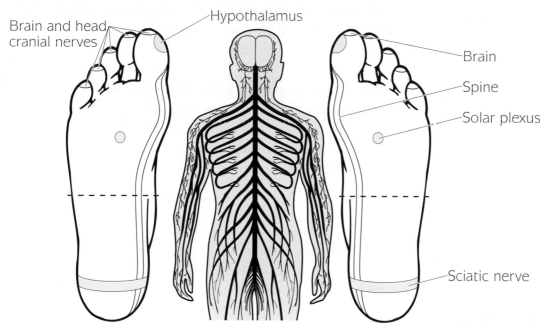

Figure 4.10 *The nervous system and the foot*

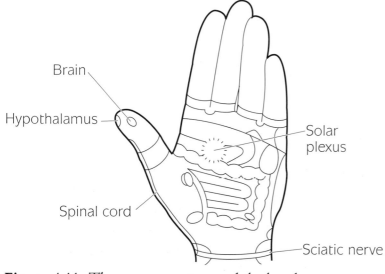

Figure 4.11 *The nervous system and the hand*

The central nervous system (CNS) consists of the brain and spinal cord. The peripheral nervous system (PNS) consists of all the nerves found outside the CNS. The autonomic nervous system (ANS) is part of the PNS and controls the involuntary movements (i.e. movements we do not have to consciously think about) of the heart, glands and smooth muscles (as found in the digestive tract). The ANS is controlled by the medulla oblongata and hypothalamus in the brain.

The solar plexus is part of the autonomic nervous system and consists of a bundle of nerves found in the abdomen at the level of the last thoracic and first lumbar vertebrae. These nerves control the activity of many organs. The solar plexus reflex is worked to help calm and relax the nervous system.

The hypothalamus controls the activities of the pituitary gland and autonomic nervous system. It controls many bodily functions including heart rate, blood pressure, movement of food through the gut, hunger and thirst, body temperature and sleeping/waking patterns. Therefore, working this reflex will help to restore homeostasis.

Dermatomes (Derma = skin, tome = thin segment)

Certain nerves correspond to certain areas of the skin and body. These specific areas are known as dermatomes. If a client suffers discomfort around the abdominal area, you could work the thoracic spine region as the nerves responsible for sensations in the abdominal area originate from the thoracic region of the spine. If a client has a problem and discomfort in the leg, you could work the nerves coming from the lumbar region as these nerves supply the leg. If an area of skin is stimulated and there is no response, it may be due to damage to the nerve supplying the dermatome.

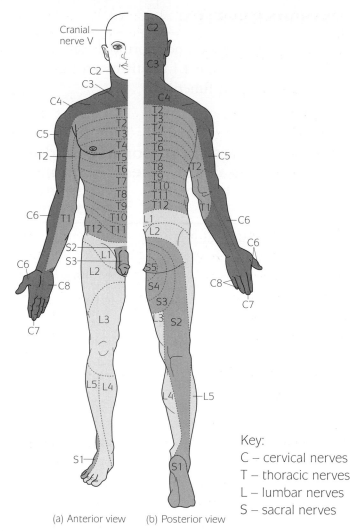

Key:
C – cervical nerves
T – thoracic nerves
L – lumbar nerves
S – sacral nerves

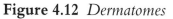
(a) Anterior view   (b) Posterior view

Figure 4.12 *Dermatomes*

Effects of reflexology on the nervous system

◆ It helps to soothe pain as endorphins are released.

◆ Working the brain will affect the whole nervous system.

◆ Working the solar plexus may help to improve the function of many organs.

◆ It helps to balance the actions of the sympathetic and parasympathetic nervous systems.

ENDOCRINE SYSTEM

The endocrine system sends hormones around the body to deliver messages. Table 4.1 briefly lists the glands and hormones and their functions.

Table 4.1 The endocrine system

Endocrine glands	Hormone released	Target organ or organs affected by hormone	What does hormone control or stimulate production of?
Anterior pituitary	Adrenocorticotropic hormone (ACTH)	Adrenal glands	Controls activity of adrenal cortex
	Thyrotrophic hormone (TSH)	Thyroid gland	Controls activity of thyroid gland
	Growth hormone	All organs	Controls growth of skeleton, muscles and organs
	Prolactin	Breasts	Stimulates milk production
	Follicle stimulating hormone (FSH)	Ovaries and testes	Stimulates the development of eggs and production of oestrogen in females. In males it stimulates sperm production
	Luteinising hormone (LH)	Ovaries and testes	Stimulates egg release from ovaries and production of progesterone. In males it stimulates the testes to make testosterone
Posterior pituitary	Anti-diuretic hormone	Kidneys	Controls water balance in the body
	Oxytocin	Breasts	Releases milk from breasts during suckling

If the outer third of the eyebrows are missing it could be a sign of an under-active thyroid gland

Table 4.2 Glands and hormones

Endocrine gland	Hormone released	Action of hormone
Pineal	Melatonin, seratonin	Helps to control body rhythms Seratonin helps to lift the mood
Thyroid	Thyroxine	Controls the metabolism, therefore affects the rate at which the body burns calories and our energy levels
Parathyroid	Parathormone	Controls calcium levels in the blood. Calcium is needed for muscle contraction and the transmission of impulses through nerves
Thymus	Thymosin	Involved with the production of lymphocytes
Adrenal cortex	Sex corticoids	Controls changes in males and females during puberty
	Glucocorticoids	Helps regulate nutrient levels in the blood. Cortisol helps to reduce inflammation and has anti-allergenic properties. Cortisol also helps to maintain the health and functioning of the cardiovascular system

Table 4.2 (continued)

Endocrine gland	Hormone released	Action of hormone
	Mineral corticoids	Helps maintain the balance of minerals in the body. Helps to control fluid balance in the body
Adrenal medulla	Adrenaline and noradrenaline	Prepares body for fight or flight response
Pancreas	Insulin and glucagon	Controls sugar levels in the blood
Ovaries	Oestrogen and progesterone	Controls female secondary sexual characteristics such as breasts, curves and pubic hair
Testes	Testosterone	Controls male secondary sexual characteristics such as bodily hair, deep voice and muscular development

Effects of reflexology on the endocrine system

Note

Human growth hormone is released during the night and triggers proteins to build new cells and repair any damage.

- When the body is under stress, certain hormones are stimulated, especially from the adrenal glands. Reflexology can help to reduce the amount of stress hormones released as it helps to reduce stress and promote relaxation in the body.

- If the menstrual cycle is irregular due to the effects of stress, reflexology can help to regulate periods as it helps to rebalance and maintain homeostasis, and de-stress the body.

- Reflexology helps to balance the output of hormones so will be helpful for many hormone-related conditions.

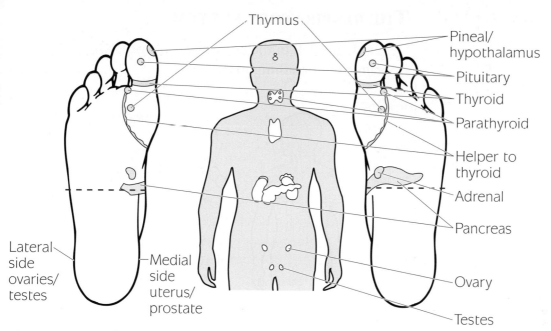

Figure 4.13 *Endocrine glands and the foot*

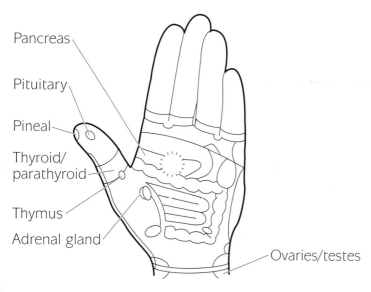

Figure 4.14 *Endocrine glands and the hand*

THE RESPIRATORY SYSTEM

Every living cell in the body needs oxygen, which we obtain from breathing in the air.

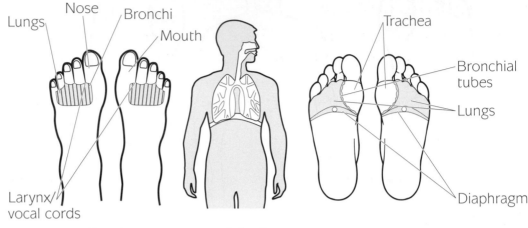

Figure 4.15 *Respiratory organs and the feet*

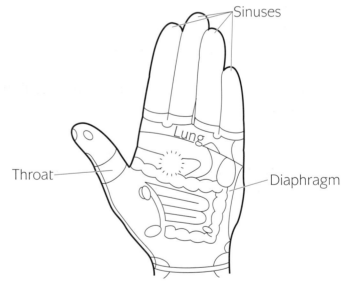

Figure 4.16 *Respiratory organs and the hands*

Effects of reflexology on the respiratory system

♦ Reflexology helps to relax the chest muscles and so breathing may be improved, especially if the client suffers with tightness in the chest often associated with anxiety problems.

- It will increase the blood circulation to the lung tissue, helping to bring nutrients and rid the body of carbon dioxide. This will improve the condition of the lungs.

- Working the diaphragm can have a deeply relaxing effect on the whole body.

- It helps to unblock sinuses and reduce inflammation, therefore helping with conditions such as sinusitis.

Note

According to Chinese medicine, the lungs are affected by both anxiety and grief. If your client is suffering from these emotions, pay particular attention to the lung reflexes on the feet.

DIGESTION

The digestive system changes the food we eat into small, simple molecules that can be absorbed into the bloodstream and used by the body to produce energy or as building materials for repair or growth.

Food contains substances called nutrients that are found within five basic food groups: protein, carbohydrates, fats, vitamins and minerals. Although fibre is not nutritionally valuable it is important for a healthy diet. All foods contain some nutrients, but hardly any food contains them all. For the body to remain healthy a variety of foods need to be eaten.

Table 4.3 Food groups

Food group	Function	Good sources
Protein	Vital for growth and repair of body's cells	Meat, fish, eggs, milk, cheese
Carbohydrates	Provide energy for the body	Potatoes, bread, sugar, cereals, pasta
Fats	Provide energy for the body	Butter, lard, vegetable oil, cheese
Vitamins/minerals	Essential for growth and general health	Fruit and vegetables
Fibre	Helps keep the muscles of the intestines exercised and provides bulk to satisfy the appetite. Helps prevent constipation	Vegetables, fruit, cereals and wholemeal foods

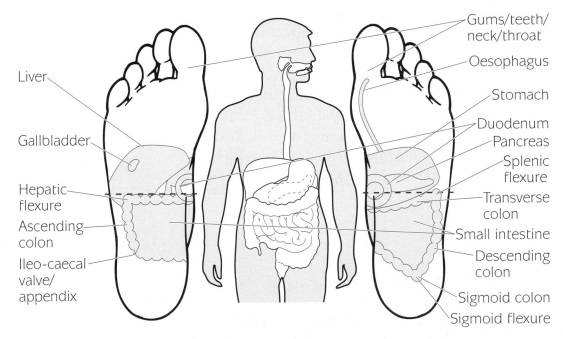

Figure 4.17 *Digestive organs and the foot*

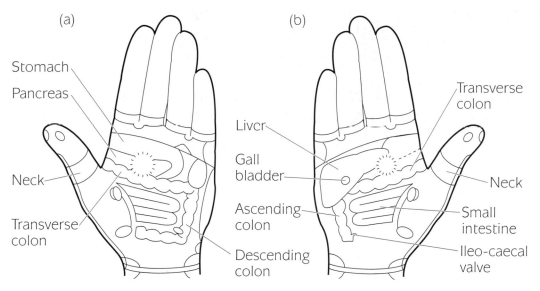

(a)

Stomach

Pancreas

Liver

Gall
bladder

Neck

Ascending
colon

Transverse
colon

Descending
colon

(b)

Transverse
colon

Neck

Small
intestine

Ileo-caecal
valve

Figure 4.18 *Digestive organs and the hands*

The digestive system

The digestive tract is more than 10 metres long; it begins
at the mouth and ends at the anus. Food takes an average
of 24 hours to pass through the digestive tract.

The small intestine is about 7 metres long and is the main
area for digestion and absorption of food into the
bloodstream. The food particles are absorbed through tiny
projections called villi. The first part of the small intestine
is known as the duodenum and it is followed by the
jejunum and the ileum. Antibiotics, drugs, alcohol and a
high intake of sugar can cause the cells of the villi to
inflame and widen, allowing unwanted food substances to
pass into the bloodstream. This can cause food intolerances
and lead to headaches, tiredness, skin problems and
arthritic types of pain in muscle and bone.

During a reflexology treatment you will work the ileo-
caecal valve, which is located very close to the appendix. It
prevents waste matter from passing back up into the small
intestine. It is an area that can easily become inflamed, as
bacteria and parasites often stick to the walls. If
inflammation occurs over a long time, this valve may stay

open, allowing toxic matter into the ileum, where it may be absorbed into the bloodstream and is a frequent cause of fatigue, headaches, nausea and generally feeling unwell.

The colon, also known as the large intestine or bowel, consists of the ascending colon which turns at the hepatic flexure to become the transverse colon. Another intestinal turn is the splenic flexure, which leads to the descending colon. It then makes an 'S' turn, forming the sigmoid flexure part of the sigmoid colon until finally becoming the rectum.

The liver deals with medication and alcohol. An individual's liver reflex may feel congested and need support if medication is taken or if excess alcohol is consumed.

Note

According to traditional Chinese medicine, the liver and gall bladder are associated with anger, and excess anger can damage the liver. If there is congestion or sensitivity in this area of the foot, it could be that your client is feeling angry about something. Also the stomach is the organ of sympathy. If a person is upset, the stomach may also become upset.

Effects of reflexology on the digestive system

◆ Reflexology on the abdomen area of the foot helps to stimulate peristalsis and promote the movement of waste matter through the colon.

◆ It helps to relieve flatulence and constipation.

◆ Reflexology over the abdomen area of the foot can help to soothe nerves and so relieve intestinal spasm associated with conditions such as irritable bowel syndrome.

THE REPRODUCTIVE SYSTEMS

The reproductive systems of males and females enable new human life to be created. This can only happen when a woman's ovum (egg) is fertilised by a man's sperm.

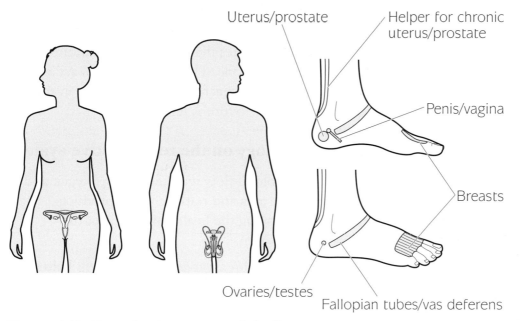

Figure 4.19 *Reproductive organs and the foot*

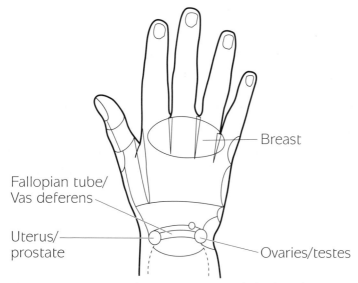

Figure 4.20 *Reproductive organs and the hands*

Male reproductive system

The testes are two oval glands and the vas deferens passes from the testes to the urethra. The prostate lies under the bladder and often enlarges in middle-aged men.

Female reproductive system

The female has two ovaries that release the hormones oestrogen and progesterone. The fallopian tubes act as a passageway for sperm to reach the ovum and it is in the fallopian tubes that the ovum is fertilised.

Effects of reflexology on the reproductive system

- The increased blood flow will help bring oxygen and nutrients to the area and remove waste products, therefore improving the health of organs of the reproductive system.

- Reflexology to the breast area of the foot will help to improve lymph drainage and so reduce fluid retention, common around the time of menstruation.

URINARY SYSTEM

The urinary system filters the blood and produces urine to ensure the body gets rid of unwanted substances that could be harmful. It consists of two kidneys, two ureters, the bladder and the urethra.

The kidneys filter the blood to remove harmful waste and toxins, so they are important in helping the body detoxify.

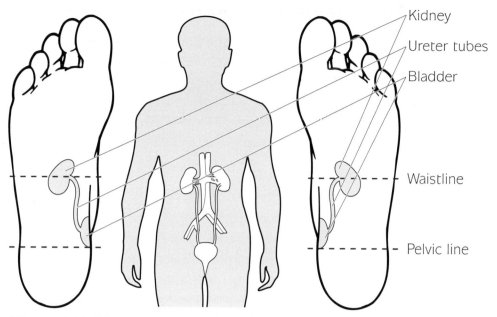

Figure 4.21 *Urinary organs and the foot*

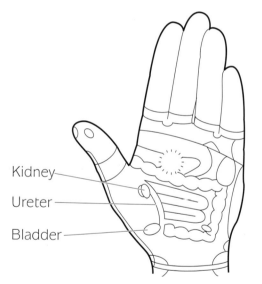

Figure 4.22 *Urinary organs and the hands*

Effects of reflexology on the urinary system

● The increased lymphatic flow may cause more urine to pass to the bladder.

● It helps to improve the functioning of the kidneys and bladder.

Note

While working on a particular area of the foot remember that organs, vessels and glands overlap, so you will probably be working over more than one reflex point.

Task 4.1

Table 4.4 Association between reflexes and systems

System	Reflexes
Skeletal	
Muscular	All muscles will be worked over during reflexology treatment.
Circulatory	
Lymphatic	
Nervous	
Endocrine	
Respiratory	
Digestive	
Reproductive	
Urinary	

Complete the table by listing all of the reflexes that are associated with each system. Look at the foot chart to help you. Some systems will have many reflexes and others will have few.

TREATMENT TECHNIQUES USING THUMBS AND FINGERS

While carrying out a reflexology treatment you will be working on the feet using your thumb and fingers. There are various techniques you can use to help work the reflex points and these include thumb walking, thumb circles, hook-in-back-up, rotation, pivot on a point and stroking.

Thumb walk/finger walking, also known as caterpillar movement

Place the pad of the thumb or finger onto the skin and press onto the body. Slide the thumb/finger forward slightly and apply pressure once again.

Thumb circles

Place the pad of thumb onto the skin, apply pressure and create a circular movement. Slide the thumb a small distance from the area worked and repeat this movement.

Hook-in-back-up

This technique helps you to work accurately on a reflex point that is deep or very small. Use the medial corner of the thumb to apply pressure. Push the thumb into the skin and slightly hook in and pull the thumb back slightly. This technique can be used to work the following reflexes: pituitary, pineal, ileo-caecal valve, appendix and sigmoid colon.

Rotation

The thumbs or fingers can be used for this technique. Place the tip of the thumb onto a reflex point and rotate onto it.

Pivot on a point

Use one hand to hold the dorsal surface of the foot and place the thumb of the other hand onto the reflex point. Use the hand to push the foot onto the thumb. Lightly rotate the foot. This technique may be used to work the diaphragm, solar plexus and the adrenal gland reflexes.

Thumb/finger stroking

Use the thumb/fingers to stroke and apply light pressure over an area. This technique is useful to help detect areas of hardness, hot/cold regions, gritty and congested areas etc. in the feet. See Chapter 7 for further information.

MASSAGE TECHNIQUES

A massage will be given to the feet at the beginning and end of the treatment. It will consist of effleurage and petrissage massage movements.

Effleurage techniques include stroking and effleurage.

Stroking

Stroking is a gentle and slow movement (like when you stroke a cat or dog) and involves the smooth gliding of the hands over a body part. It is mostly a restful movement, ideal to use at the beginning or the end of the massage. One or both hands can be used and either the palm of the hand or tips of the fingers or thumbs can perform this movement.

Effects of stroking

- Induces relaxation.
- Calms the nerves.
- Lightly stimulates blood circulation.
- Lightly stimulates lymphatic circulation.

Uses of stroking

- To calm and relax.
- To create erythema and warm up an area.

Effleurage

Effleurage is similar, although it is a deeper movement than stroking and is usually performed slowly. Effleurage can be superficially or deeply applied to the body. The

Note

Finger/thumb stroking can be used over the intestine reflexes to help prevent or treat constipation.

hands may be used alternately or both together to perform this massage movement. The hands must relax completely and mould to the shape of the limb or part being treated.

Effleurage should be carried out in the same direction as blood travels in the veins, known as venous return (e.g. effleurage should be applied in an upward direction on the legs and arms, in the direction of the heart). At the end of the movement the hands glide back using almost no pressure at all.

On areas such as the fingers and toes, the pads of the fingertips or thumb may be used to effleurage the area.

> **Note**
>
> Effleurage is a French word that means 'stroking'.

Effects of effleurage on the body

- Promotes relaxation.
- Has a soothing effect on the nerves.
- Increases blood flow.
- Increases lymphatic flow.
- Stimulates the sebaceous glands.
- Stimulates the sweat glands.

Uses of effleurage

- To begin and end massage on a body part.
- To warm the skin and prepare the muscles for deeper work (similar to a warm-up prior to undertaking exercise).
- To link one massage movement to another to help the massage flow smoothly.
- To help spread the oil or cream over the area to be massaged.
- To promote relaxation.
- To improve lymphatic and venous (blood in veins) drainage.
- To encourage the removal of toxins.

Petrissage

Note

Petrissage is a French word that means 'kneading'.

Petrissage movements use deeper pressure than those used for effleurage and are useful for working deep into the muscle tissue. These movements usually involve pressing the muscle against the bone or lifting it away from the bone. Massage movements for this group include kneading and frictions.

Effects of petrissage on the body

♦ Petrissage increases blood circulation. Therefore it brings fresh blood, containing oxygen and nutrients, to the area and removes waste products such as lactic acid that may be the cause of stiffness and discomfort in a muscle.

♦ It increases lymphatic flow so waste products and tissue fluid are removed more quickly. This will help with fluid retention (oedema).

♦ Increased blood supply to the skin causes the cells in the basal layer to regenerate. As the cells divide they push upwards towards the surface of the skin. The dead skin cells of the horny layer will shed (desquamation) giving the skin a better texture and healthier look.

Uses of petrissage

♦ Petrissage helps relieve stiffness and pain in muscles as waste products are removed from the affected area.

♦ It stimulates poor blood circulation.

♦ It stimulates lymphatic drainage thereby relieving fluid retention (oedema).

♦ It relaxes tense muscles.

Types of petrissage movements

There are different types of petrissage movements and these include palmar kneading, thumb kneading and finger kneading.

- Palmar kneading: the palm of one hand (single handed) or both (double handed) is/are used to create fairly deep circular movements. The pressure is mainly applied during the upward part of the circle. It is a good movement to use on the sole of the foot.

- Thumb kneading: the pads of the thumbs are used to perform fairly deep and small circular movements. This technique helps you feel, locate and treat congestion within the foot.

- Finger kneading: the pads of the fingers are used to create fairly deep, small, circular movements. Finger kneading is particularly useful around the joints of the ankles.

Note

Massage is very relaxing and helps to induce feelings of calmness and well-being.

5 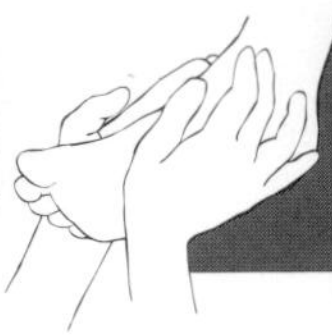

Giving a reflexology treatment

FOOT MASSAGE

Foot massage is used at the beginning of the treatment to relax the client and prepare the foot for further work. It allows you to assess the feet through observation and touch.

Powder, oil and creams

Therapists often use powder to carry out the reflexology treatment as they feel they can access the reflexes more easily than by using oils and creams. Apply talc-free powder, arrowroot or a suitable substitute. There are also specialist powders for reflexology. Shake a little onto the hand before applying to the feet. Oil or cream can be used to massage the feet towards the end of the treatment.

Prior to treatment

Before giving a treatment it is important that you:

- wash your hands
- check the feet, ankles and lower legs for signs of any contraindications
- ensure the feet are clean. Baby wipes are ideal as they are effective at cleansing but are also gentle on the skin
- ensure you have everything at hand: paperwork, rolled-up towels etc. A foot map should be used to locate any areas of sensitivity or congestion
- observe the feet and use a foot map to note areas of hard skin, moles and bunions etc. (see Figure 7.1, Chapter 7).

PROTECTING YOURSELF FROM NEGATIVE ENERGIES

Have you ever spent time with someone and felt drained and exhausted after they left? You probably took on some of their emotional baggage and allowed their negative energies to affect you. Negative energy may be emitted from the client and it will affect their aura. As both of your auras will overlap, it is possible that you could absorb some of this negative energy.

To help prevent this occurring when carrying out a reflexology treatment, you can visualise yourself surrounded in a bubble of light. This light will help protect you from any negative energy that may be given off by your client and which would drain your energy levels. Crystals and stones, such as amber, borite or sugilite, are also useful for this purpose and can be placed nearby for protection. At the end of the session hold your hands under cool running water and imagine negative energies trickling away with the water.

GROUNDING

To prepare you for the reflexology treatment it is helpful to ground yourself so that you can concentrate and focus on giving an excellent treatment. It will help to connect you to the earth and its energy. Grounding can be done in various ways which include imagining that roots, like tree roots, are growing from the bottom of your feet into the ground. Crystals such as haematite and tiger eye (gold) will help to keep you grounded and can be placed nearby while giving treatment.

REFLEXOLOGY ROUTINE

The following routine is a suggested sequence which will take around 50 minutes to carry out. If the client is suffering from a chronic condition, you should pay particular attention to the relevant reflex and also work the chronic reflex (e.g. if the client is suffering from chronic sciatica, you should work the sciatic reflex and the chronic sciatic reflex).

The routine commonly begins on the client's right foot. When the right foot has been treated it is covered with a towel and treatment begins on the left foot.

Why begin on the right foot?

The right side of the brain controls the left side of the body and vice versa. Beginning the treatment on the right foot rebalances the physical first (the left side of the brain, which deals with logic and analysis) before moving on to the emotional side (the right side of the brain, which deals with creativity and intuition). Working the right foot first also follows the natural flow of the colon, the reflex for which starts on the right foot and ends on the left.

Foot massage

Firstly place your left hand on the client's right foot and you right hand on the client's left foot and hold for a few moments. Begin the massage on the client's right foot.

1 **Stroking/effleurage to foot**
   Place one hand on the dorsal surface of the foot and the other on the bottom of the foot. With the foot sandwiched between the hands stroke the whole foot.

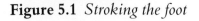

Figure 5.1 *Stroking the foot*

2 Rotate foot in both directions

Hold the foot firmly with one hand and the heel with the other. Rotate the foot clockwise and anticlockwise four times.

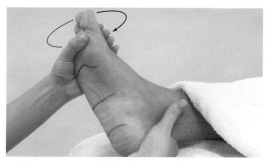

Figure 5.2 *Rotate foot*

Note

This movement helps to loosen the hip joints and lumbar spine.

3 Finger circles (kneading) to ankle

Use the pads of the fingers of both hands to create small circles around the ankle.

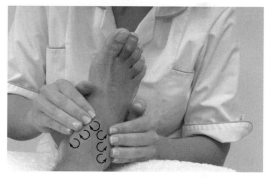

Figure 5.3 *Finger circles to ankle*

4 Thumb stroke to dorsal side of foot

Hold onto the foot with both hands, fingers underneath each side of the foot and the thumbs placed just above the toes. Stroke the thumbs upwards and over the dorsal surface of the foot.

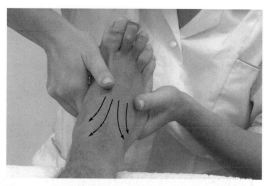

Figure 5.4 *Thumb stroke to dorsal side of foot*

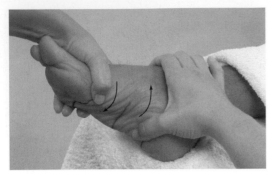

Figure 5.5 *Spinal twist*

5 Spinal twist

With both hands side by side, sandwich the medial part of the foot between the fingers and thumb. Alternately move the hands to produce a twisting, wringing action. Work from the ankles towards the toes.

Note

You will be loosening tension in the spinal muscles with the spinal twist movement.

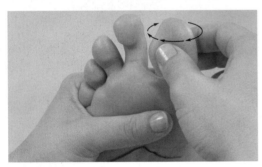

Figure 5.6 *Toe twirling and stretch*

6 Toe twirling and stretch

Hold the foot with one hand and a toe between your finger and thumb. Twist the toe clockwise and anticlockwise four times and then gently stretch. Ensure all the toes are worked.

Note

You will be loosening the muscles in the neck with this movement (Fig 5.6).

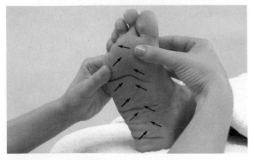

Figure 5.7 *Thumb stroke to bottom of foot (zigzag)*

7 Thumb stroke to bottom of foot (zigzag)

Place the fingers of both hands on the dorsal surface of the foot. Position the thumbs on the bottom of the foot below the toes. Use the thumbs to alternately stroke the foot in a zigzag motion. Repeat this movement until the whole of the bottom of the foot has been worked.

8 Palm of hand circles to bottom of the foot

Place one hand on the dorsal surface of the foot to support it and the other hand on the bottom of the foot. Use the palm of this hand to make circular movements; ensure the whole of the bottom of the foot is worked.

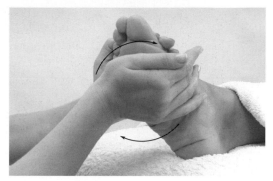

Figure 5.8 *Palm of hand circles to bottom of the foot*

9 Pull and push to foot (flex and extend)

Hold the heel with one hand and gently push the foot down (this will stretch out the chest area on the foot). Now push the foot back so that the Achilles tendon is stretched.

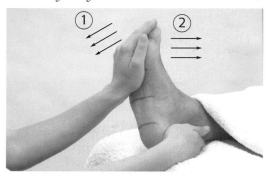

Figure 5.9 *Pull and push to foot (flex and extend)*

10 Stroking/effleurage to foot

Place one hand on the dorsal surface of the foot and the other on the bottom of the foot. With the foot sandwiched between the hands stroke the whole foot.

Reflexology routine

Begin on the client's right foot.

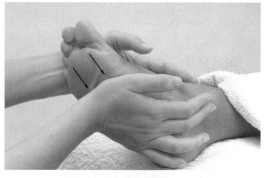

Figure 5.10 *Stroking to foot*

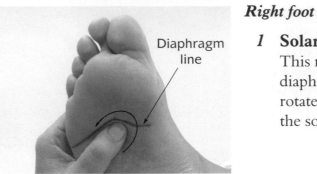

Figure 5.11 *Solar plexus*

Right foot

1 Solar plexus

This reflex is located around zone 2 below the diaphragm line. Use the thumb to either rotate or use the pivot on a point technique to the solar plexus reflex for about four seconds.

Note

To find the solar plexus squeeze the foot; there will be an indent to indicate the position of this reflex. Working this reflex will help to calm and relax the client.

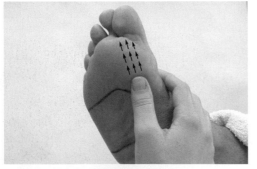

Figure 5.12a *Thyroid/helper to thyroid (1)*

2 Thyroid/helper to thyroid

Found in zones 1 and 2. Begin at diaphragm and work up towards the big toe. Repeat this movement until the whole area is worked. Now work in rows from medial to lateral across the foot.

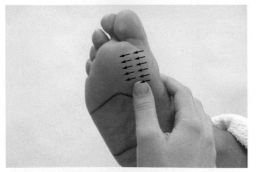

Figure 5.12b *Thyroid/helper to thyroid (2)*

3 Parathyroid

Use your index finger and thumb to press on the area between the big toe and second toe, and rotate for about four seconds.

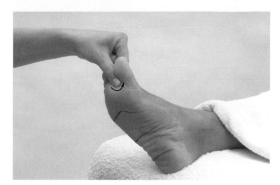

Figure 5.13 *Parathyroid*

4 Thymus

Found halfway between the parathyroid and diaphragm. Press and rotate for about four seconds.

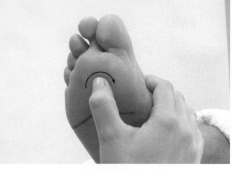

Figure 5.14 *Thymus*

5 Back and side of neck

Found at the base of the big toe. Thumb walk in rows from medial to lateral ensuring the whole area is covered.

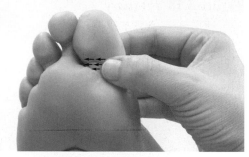

Figure 5.15 *Back and side of neck*

6 Head

Begin at the base of the big toe and work in rows up the toe until you reach the lateral side of the big toe. Now thumb walk medial to lateral across the big toe.

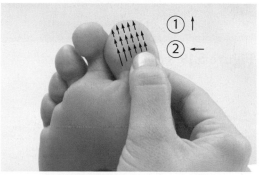

Figure 5.16 *Head*

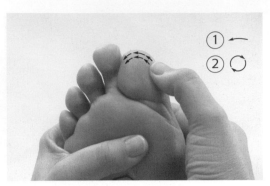

Figure 5.17 *Brain*

7 Brain

Work over the top of the big toe using thumb walking and then thumb circles.

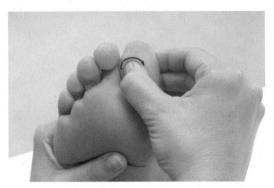

Figure 5.18 *Pituitary*

8 Pituitary

Find the middle of the whorl of the fingerprint. Use the medial edge of the thumb or the knuckle to rotate onto it or alternatively use the hook-in-back-up technique.

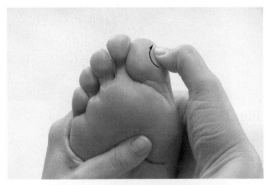

Figure 5.19 *Hypothalamus/pineal*

9 Hypothalamus/pineal

Press the thumb onto the medial edge of the big toe and rotate onto it.

10 Face, teeth and front of neck

Use the first two fingers to walk across the front of the big toe. Begin at the base of the nail and work in rows across the big toe.

Figure 5.20 *Face, teeth and front of neck*

11 Sinuses

Found on the top of the toes. Thumb walk up and over each toe in rows then slide up and over each toe to drain the sinuses.

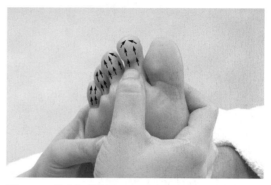

Figure 5.21 *Sinuses*

12 Eye, ear and eustachian tube

Found between zones 2 and 4. Gently pull the toes back. Thumb walk across the area at the base of the toes. Work from lateral to medial and then back the other way.

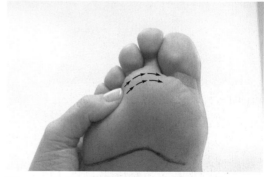

Figure 5.22 *Eye, ear and eustachian tube*

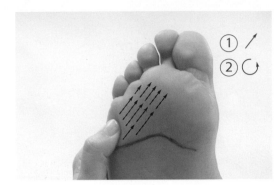

Figure 5.23 *Shoulder*

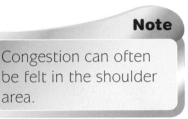

Note

Congestion can often be felt in the shoulder area.

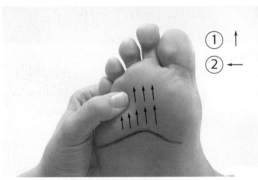

Figure 5.24 *Lungs*

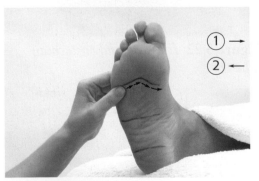

Figure 5.25 *Diaphragm*

13 Shoulder

Found around zones 3, 4 and 5. Thumb walk and then thumb circle over whole shoulder area.

14 Lungs

Found between zones 2 and 5. Gently push back the toes. Begin at the diaphragm and thumb walk up over the chest area. Then work from medial to lateral across the chest area.

15 Diaphragm

Found lying in all zones and separates the chest and abdomen. Thumb walk or pivot on a point from medial to lateral and then use the other thumb to work back the other way.

16 Liver

Found between zones 2 to 5 between the diaphragm and waistline. Thumb walk across the liver diagonally and use the other thumb to work back the other way. Thumb circling onto this reflex is also very effective.

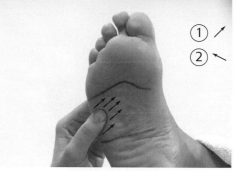

Figure 5.26 *Liver*

17 Gall bladder

Found in zone 3 about 1 cm below the diaphragm. Press and rotate onto the area with the thumb.

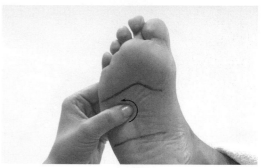

Figure 5.27 *Gall bladder*

Note

While working this reflex with the thumb, place the middle finger on the dorsal surface of the foot so that the finger and thumb could touch if they could penetrate the foot. This is known as linking and will help stimulate energy flow.

18 Stomach/pancreas

Found between zones 1 and 2 of the right foot between the diaphragm and waistline. Thumb walk from medial to lateral and use the other thumb to walk back the other way.

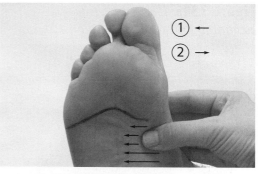

Figure 5.28 *Stomach/pancreas*

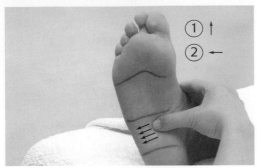

Figure 5.29 *Small intestine*

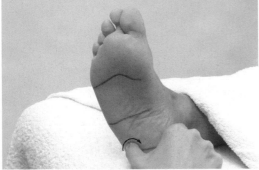

Figure 5.30 *Ileo-caecal valve*

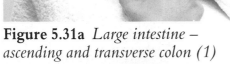

Figure 5.31a *Large intestine –
ascending and transverse colon (1)*

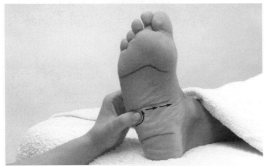

Figure 5.31b *Large intestine –
ascending and transverse colon (2)*

19 Small intestine

Found below the waistline and between zones
2 and 4. Use the thumb to work over the area
beginning in an upward direction towards the
toes and then work across the foot.

20 Ileo-caecal valve

Found between zones 4 and 5, about 4 cm
from the heel, near to the pelvic line. Use the
thumb to rotate onto the area; alternatively use
the hook-in-back-up technique for about four
seconds.

21 Large intestine – ascending and transverse colon

Thumb walk up ascending colon (found mainly
in zone 4), rotate onto the hepatic flexure, and
walk across transverse colon to zone 1.

22 Kidney and ureter

Gently pull back the toes to find the tendon in zone 2. The kidney will be found along the waistline around zones 2 and 3. Use the thumb to work over the kidney in different directions and then work along the ureter towards the bladder.

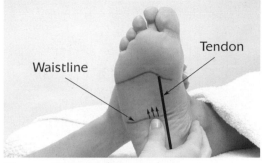

Figure 5.32 *Kidney and ureter*

23 Bladder

The bladder is found in zone 1 and is often circular in shape and slightly protrudes on the foot. Work over the bladder in different directions.

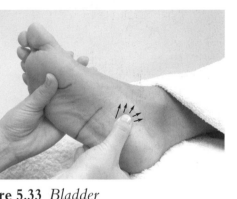

Figure 5.33 *Bladder*

24 Adrenal gland

The adrenal gland is found above the kidney, located halfway between the diaphragm and waistline in zone 1. Use the thumb to hook in, press and rotate for about four seconds. The pivot-on-a-point technique may also be used.

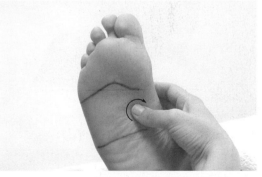

Figure 5.34 *Adrenal gland*

> **Note**
>
> This gland will often feel sensitive to the client, especially if they are stressed.

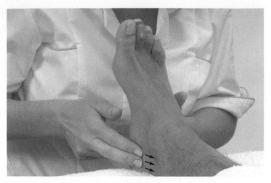

Figure 5.35 *Pelvic area*

25 Pelvic area

Found between the ankle bone (medial side) and the bottom of the heel. Use the fingers or thumb to work in rows over the reflex area.

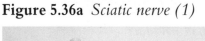

Figure 5.36a *Sciatic nerve (1)*

26 Sciatic nerve

Use the thumb or knuckle to work medial to lateral and the other thumb to walk back the other way. Finger walk, using both hands, up each side of the ankle along the Achilles tendon.

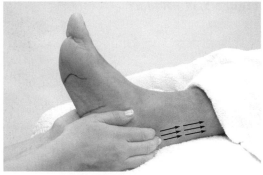

Figure 5.36b *Sciatic nerve (2)*

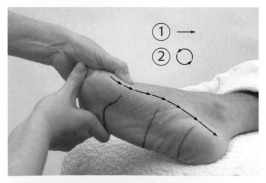

Figure 5.37 *Spine*

27 Spine

Thumb walk or use the pads of the first two fingers to work along the spine. Work across it once again but this time rotate onto each vertebra.

28 Spinal nerves and muscles

Thumb walk across the spine rather than along it. Thumb walk from the cervical spine to the coccyx in rows.

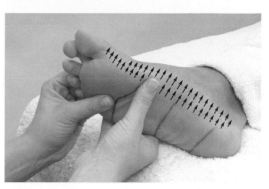

Figure 5.38 *Spinal nerves and muscles*

29 Uterus/prostate

Found midway on a diagonal from the ankle bone (medial side) to the base of the heel. Use the thumb to press and rotate onto the area.

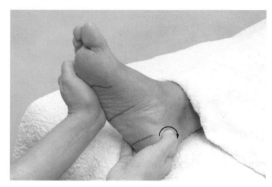

Figure 5.39 *Uterus/prostate*

Note

Work lightly on the uterus area if the client is in the first two days of her period.

30 Uterus, prostate, rectum, sciatic (if condition is chronic)

Use the fingers and thumb to press either side of the Achilles tendon.

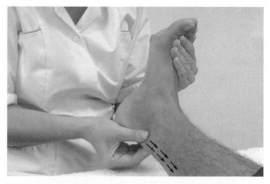

Figure 5.40 *Uterus, prostate, rectum, sciatic (if condition is chronic)*

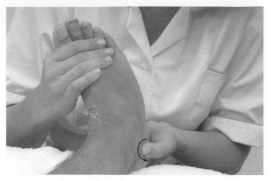

Figure 5.41 *Ovary/testes*

31 Ovary/testes

Find the area midway between the ankle bone (lateral side) and the base of the heel. Press and rotate with the thumb or finger.

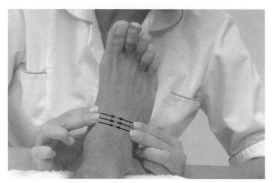

Figure 5.42 *Fallopian tubes/vas deferens*

32 Fallopian tubes/vas deferens

Use the first two fingers of each hand to work across the dorsal surface of the foot. Repeat the movement twice.

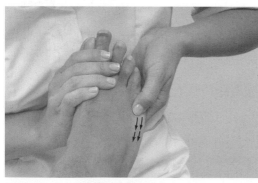

Figure 5.43 *Shoulder, upper arms, elbow, lower arm, wrist*

33 Shoulder, upper arms, elbow, lower arm, wrist

Thumb walk along the lateral side of the foot.

34 Hip/thigh/knee

Use the first two fingers to create circles around the ankle bone for the hip reflex. Use the thumb or fingers to work along the foot towards the knee reflex. Then rotate onto the knee reflex.

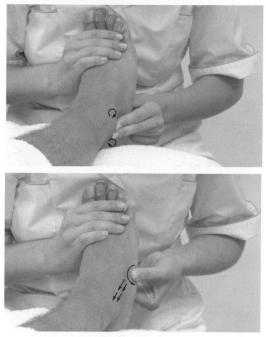

Figure 5.44 *Hip/thigh/knee*

35 Chronic back helper area/lower back/sacroiliac joint and pelvis (if condition is chronic)

Thumb walk in rows over the lateral side of the heel area and then use the other thumb to work back the other way.

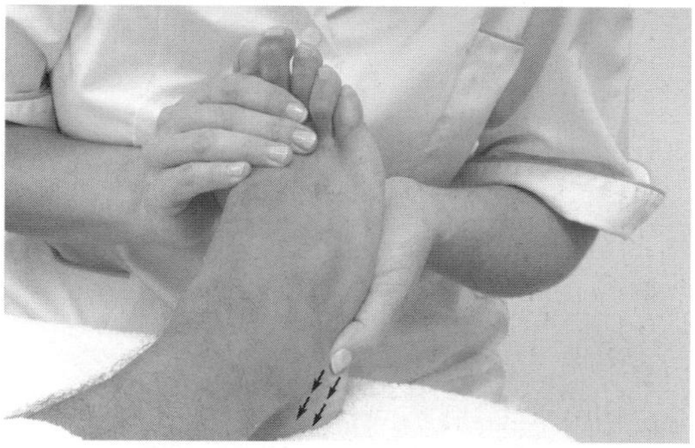

Figure 5.45 *Chronic back helper area/lower back/sacroiliac joint and pelvis (if condition is chronic)*

Note

The sacrum is joined to the hip bone to form the sacroiliac joint.

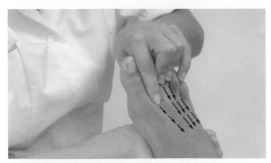

Figure 5.46 *Lymphatic*

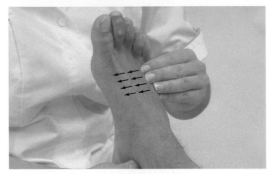

Figure 5.47 *Chest/breast area*

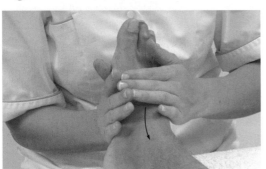

Figure 5.48 *Stroking*

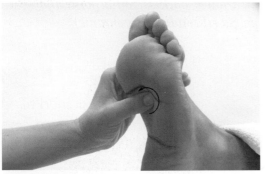

Figure 5.49 *Solar plexus*

36 Lymphatic

Begin at the web between the first two toes and use the finger or thumb to walk along each zone towards the wrist. Then slide the fingers over the same area to help lymphatic drainage.

37 Chest/breast area

Use the first three fingers to work in rows across the dorsal surface of the foot. Then use the fingers of the other hand to work back the other way.

38 Stroking

Sandwich the foot and use both hands to stroke it. Repeat this movement four times.

Left foot

Massage the left foot before beginning the reflexology treatment. Repeat steps 1 to 10 of the massage routine.

39 Solar plexus

This reflex is located in zone 2 below the diaphragm line. Pivot on a point or use the thumb to rotate on the area for about four seconds.

40 Thyroid/helper to thyroid

Found in zone 1, begin at diaphragm and work in rows up towards the big toe. Now work in rows from medial to lateral across the foot.

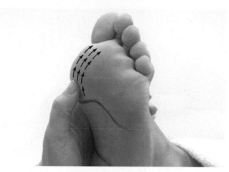

Figure 5.50a *Thyroid/helper to thyroid (1)*

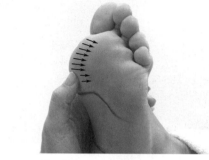

Figure 5.50b *Thyroid/helper to thyroid (2)*

41 Parathyroid

Press on the area between the big toe and second toe and rotate for about four seconds.

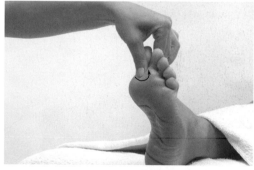

Figure 5.51 *Parathyroid*

42 Thymus

Found halfway between the parathyroid and diaphragm. Press and rotate for about four seconds.

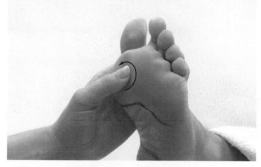

Figure 5.52 *Thymus*

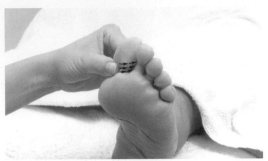

Figure 5.53 *Back of neck*

43 Back of neck
Thumb walk in rows from medial to lateral ensuring the whole area is covered.

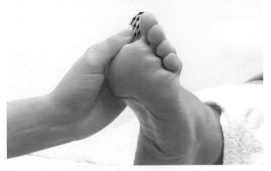

Figure 5.54 *Head*

44 Head
Begin at the base of the big toe and work in rows over the toe until you reach the lateral side of the big toe.

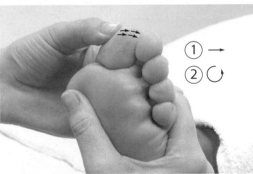

Figure 5.55 *Brain*

45 Brain
Work over the top of the big toe using thumb walking and then thumb circles.

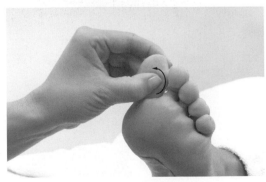

Figure 5.56 *Pituitary*

46 Pituitary
Find the middle of the whorl of the fingerprint. Use the thumb or knuckle to rotate onto it or use the hook-in-back-up technique.

47 Hypothalamus/pineal

Press the thumb to rotate onto the medial edge of the big toe or use the hook-in-back-up technique to work the pineal.

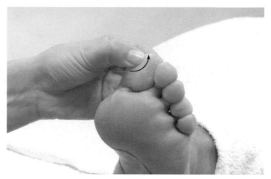

Figure 5.57 *Hypothalamus/pineal*

48 Face, teeth and front of neck

Use the first two fingers to walk across the front of the big toe. Begin at the base of the nail and work in rows down the big toe.

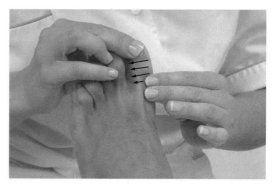

Figure 5.58 *Face, teeth and front of neck*

49 Sinuses

Found on the top of the toes. Thumb walk up and over each toe. Slide up and over each toe to drain the sinuses.

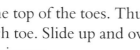

Figure 5.59 *Sinuses*

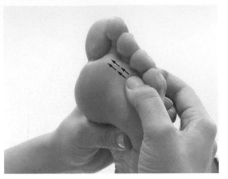

Figure 5.60 *Eye, ear and eustachian tube*

50 Eye, ear and eustachian tube
Gently pull the toes back. Thumb walk across the area at the base of the toes. Work from lateral to medial.

Figure 5.61 *Shoulder*

51 Shoulder
Found between zones 3 and 5. Thumb walk or thumb circle over whole shoulder area.

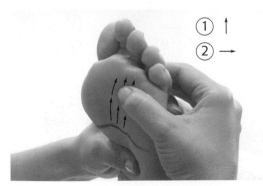

Figure 5.62 *Lungs*

52 Lungs
Found between zones 2 and 5. Gently push back the toes. Begin at the diaphragm and thumb walk in rows over the chest area. Use the other thumb to walk back the other way.

53 Heart

The heart reflex is located on the left foot in zones 1 and 2 and also on the right foot in zone 1. Thumb walk in different directions over the heart area.

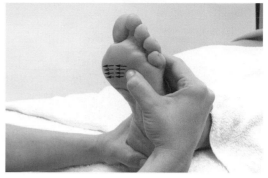

Figure 5.63 *Heart*

54 Spleen

Found under the diaphragm between zones 4 and 5. Thumb walk and then rotate on the area.

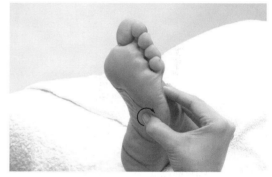

Figure 5.64 *Spleen*

55 Pancreas/stomach

Found between the diaphragm and waistline. Use the thumb to work in rows over this area, medial to lateral, and then use the other thumb to work back the other way.

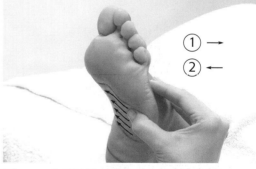

Figure 5.65 *Pancreas/stomach*

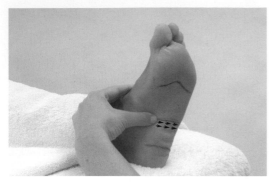

Figure 5.66a *Transverse colon*

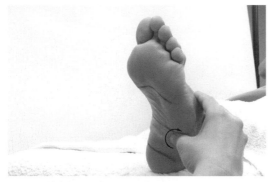

Figure 5.66b *Splenic flexure*

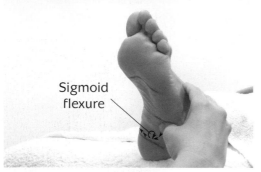

Sigmoid
flexure

Figure 5.67 *Descending colon*

Figure 5.68 *Small intestine*

56 Transverse colon

The transverse colon is found just below the waistline. Use the thumb to work across the transverse colon. Change thumbs and rotate on the splenic flexure.

57 Descending colon

Thumb walk down along the descending colon. At the sigmoid flexure press and rotate or use the hook-in-back-up technique. Work along the sigmoid colon to the rectum and anus.

58 Small intestine

Found below the transverse colon between zones 2 and 4. Use the thumb to work over the area beginning in an upward direction towards the toes and then work across the foot.

59 Kidney and ureter

Gently pull back the toes to find the tendon in zone 2. The kidney will be found around zone 2 along the waistline. Work over the kidney in different directions and then along the ureter towards the bladder.

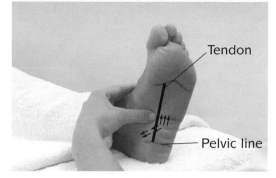

Figure 5.69 *Kidney and ureter*

60 Bladder

The bladder is often circular in shape and protrudes slightly on the foot. Work over the bladder in different directions.

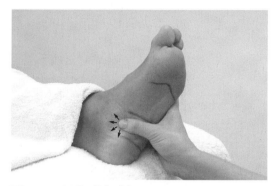

Figure 5.70 *Bladder*

61 Adrenal gland

The adrenal gland is found above the kidney halfway between the diaphragm line and waistline in zone 1. Use the thumb to hook in, press and rotate for about four seconds.

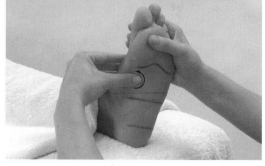

Figure 5.71 *Adrenal gland*

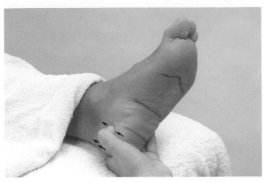

Figure 5.72 *Pelvic area*

62 Pelvic area

Found between the ankle bone (medial side) and bottom of the foot. Thumb walk in rows across the pelvic area reflex.

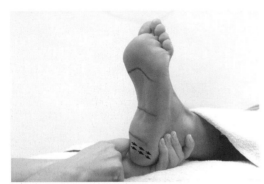

Figure 5.73a *Sciatic nerve (1)*

63 Sciatic nerve

Use the thumb or knuckle of the middle finger to work medial to lateral and the other thumb to work back the other way. Use both hands to finger walk up each side of the ankle.

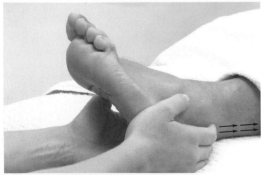

Figure 5.73b *Sciatic nerve (2)*

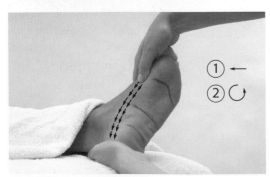

Figure 5.74 *Spine*

64 Spine

Thumb walk along the spine and then work across it again but this time rotate onto each vertebra.

65 Spinal nerves and muscles

Thumb walk in small rows from the cervical spine to the coccyx, working across the spine rather than along it.

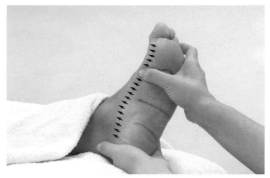

Figure 5.75 *Spinal nerves and muscles*

66 Uterus/prostate

Found midway between the medial malleolus and the heel. Use the thumb to press and rotate on the area.

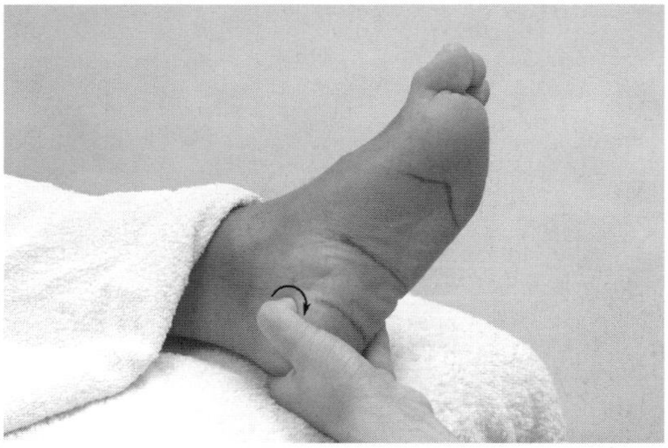

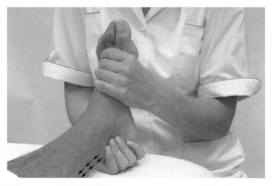

Figure 5.76 *Uterus/prostate*

67 Uterus, prostate, sciatic, rectum (if condition is chronic)

Use the finger and thumb to press up either side of the Achilles tendon.

Figure 5.77 *Uterus, prostate, sciatic, rectum (if condition is chronic)*

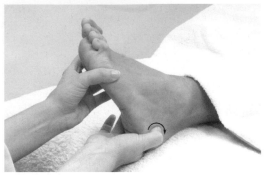

Figure 5.78 *Ovary/testes*

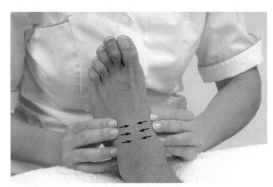

Figure 5.79 *Fallopian tubes/vas deferens*

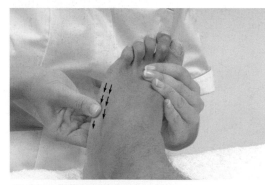

Figure 5.80 *Shoulder, upper arms, elbow, lower arm, wrist*

68 Ovary/testes

Find the area midway between the ankle bone (lateral malleolus) and the base of the heel. Press and rotate with the thumb.

69 Fallopian tubes/vas deferens

Use first two fingers of each hand to work across the dorsal surface to the top of the foot. Repeat twice.

70 Shoulder, upper arms, elbow, lower arm, wrist

Thumb walk along the lateral side of the foot.

71 Hip/thigh/knee

Use the first two fingers to create circles around the ankle bone for the hip reflex. Use the thumb or fingers to work along the foot towards the knee reflex. Then rotate onto the knee reflex.

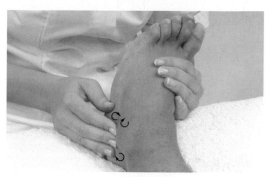

Figure 5.81a *Hip/thigh/knee (1)*

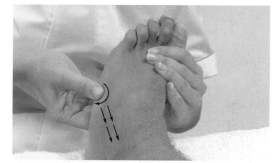

Figure 5.81b *Hip/thigh/knee (2)*

72 Chronic back helper area/lower back/sacroiliac joint and pelvis (for chronic conditions)

Thumb walk in rows over the lateral side of the heel and then work in another direction to ensure the region is covered thoroughly.

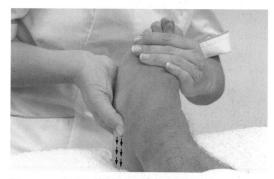

Figure 5.82 *Chronic back helper area/lower back/sacroiliac joint and pelvis (for chronic conditions)*

73 Lymphatic

Finger or thumb walk along each zone and then slide fingers over the same area to help lymphatic drainage.

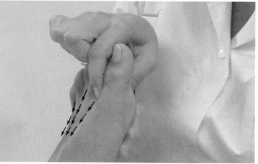

Figure 5.83 *Lymphatic*

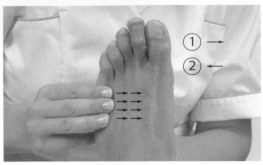

Figure 5.84 *Chest/breast area*

74 Chest/breast area
Use the first three fingers to work in rows across the dorsal surface of the foot. Then use the fingers of the other hand to work back the other way.

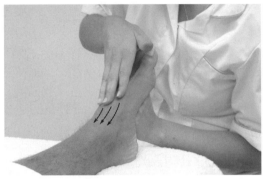

Figure 5.85 *Finger surfing*

75 Finger surfing
Sweep the fingers over the dorsal surface of the foot between the tendons towards the ankle.

Massage

Complete the treatment by massaging the feet. You may apply oil or cream if you wish. Begin on the right foot and move to the left foot.

1 Rocking
Cup the foot in both hands and move the hands back and forth so that a rocking action is caused.

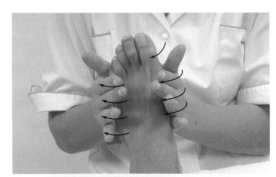

Figure 5.86a *Rocking (1)*

Figure 5.86b *Rocking (2)*

2 Hands rub to side of foot

Cup the foot in both hands and quickly rub the hands up and down each side of the foot.

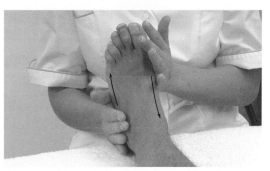

Figure 5.87a *Hands rub to side of foot (1)*

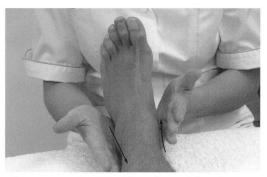

Figure 5.87b *Hands rub to side of foot (2)*

3 Fist press

Hold the foot with one hand and create a fist shape with the other. Push the fist into the chest area and work down the foot repeating this movement.

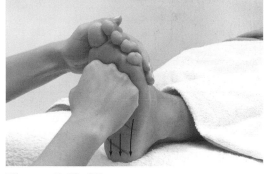

Figure 5.88 *Fist press*

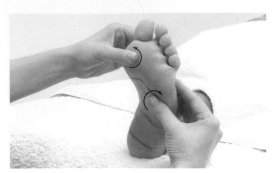

Figure 5.89 *Thumb circles to bottom of the foot*

4 Thumb circles to bottom of the foot
Place the fingers on the dorsal surface of the foot and the thumbs just beneath the toes. Use the pads of the thumbs to perform small, circular movements. Work over the whole of the bottom of the foot.

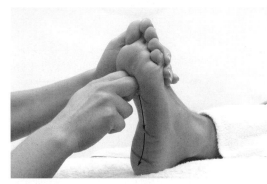

Figure 5.90a *Knuckle stroking (1)*

5 Knuckle stroking
Support the foot with one hand and create a fist shape with the other. Stroke the sole with the knuckles, working up and down the foot and then side to side.

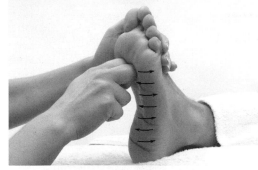

Figure 5.90b *Knuckle stroking (2)*

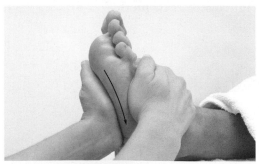

Figure 5.91 *Stroking*

6 Stroking
Sandwich the foot and use both hands to stroke it and then finger surf (see no. 75 above) on the dorsal surface of the foot. Repeat this movement four times.

After massaging both feet you can complete the treatment by giving a solar plexus press.

7 Solar plexus press

Place the thumbs on the solar plexus reflex of each foot. Press and rotate for about four seconds.

Now wrap the feet with towels to keep them warm and allow the client to rest for a short while. Perhaps you can offer them a glass of water or a herbal tea.

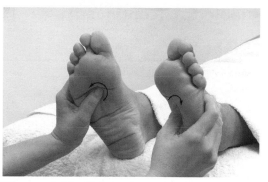

Figure 5.92 *Solar plexus press*

Reflexology routine – quick glance

Table 5.1 Reflexology routine

Right foot	Left foot
Massage	Massage
Stroking/effleurage	Stroking/effleurage
Rotation of foot	Rotation of foot
Finger circles around ankle joint	Finger circles around ankle joint
Thumb stroke to dorsal side of foot	Thumb stroke to dorsal side of foot
Spinal twist	Spinal twist
Toe twirling and stretch	Toe twirling and stretch
Thumb stroke (zigzag) to bottom of foot	Thumb stroke (zigzag) to bottom of foot
Palm of hand circles to foot	Palm of hand circles to foot
Push and pull to foot	Push and pull to foot
Stroking/effleurage	Stroking/effleurage
Reflexology treatment	Reflexology treatment
Solar plexus	Solar plexus
Thyroid/helper to thyroid	Thyroid/helper to thyroid
Parathyroid	Parathyroid
Thymus	Thymus
Back and side of neck	Back and side of neck
Head	Head

Table 5.1 (continued)

Right foot	Left foot
Brain	Brain
Pituitary	Pituitary
Hypothalamus/pineal	Hypothalamus/pineal
Face/teeth/front of neck	Face/front of neck
Sinuses	Sinuses
Eye/ear/eustachian tube	Eye/ear/eustachian tube
Shoulder	Shoulder
Lung	Lung
Diaphragm	Heart
Liver	Spleen
Gall bladder	Pancreas/stomach
Stomach/pancreas	Transverse colon
Small intestine	Descending colon
Ileo-caecal valve	Small intestine
Large intestine – ascending/transverse	Kidney/ureter
Kidney and ureter	Bladder
Bladder	Adrenal glands
Adrenal gland	Pelvic area – heel
Pelvic area – heel	Sciatic nerve
Sciatic nerve	Spine
Spine	Spinal nerves and muscles
Spinal nerves and muscles	Uterus/prostate
Uterus/prostate	Chronic uterus/prostate/sciatic/rectum
Chronic uterus/prostate/sciatic/rectum	Ovary/testes
Ovary/testes	Fallopian tubes/vas deferens
Fallopian tubes/vas deferens	Shoulder/upper arms/elbow/lower arm/wrist

Table 5.1 (continued)

Right foot	Left foot
Shoulder/upper arms/elbow/lower arm/wrist	Hip/thigh/knee
Hip/thigh/knee	Back (chronic conditions)
Back (chronic conditions)	Lymphatic
Lymphatic	Chest/breast area
Chest/breast area	Stroking/effleurage
Stroking/effleurage	Massage
Massage	Stroking/effleurage
Stroking/effleurage	Rocking
Rocking	Hands rub to side of foot
Hands rub to side of foot	Fist press
Fist press	Thumb circles to bottom of the foot
Thumb circles to bottom of the foot	Knuckle stroking
Knuckle stroking	Stroking and finger surfing
Stroking and finger surfing	Solar plexus press
Solar plexus press	

6 Hand and ear reflexology

Hand or ear reflexology can be given as a separate treatment or to complement the reflexology treatment. It is similar to foot reflexology in that the body can be mapped out on the hand and ear. Blockages and energy imbalances can be found and treated, and so energy flow can be restored.

HAND REFLEXOLOGY

The hand reflexology treatment will take about 30 minutes.

Task 6.1

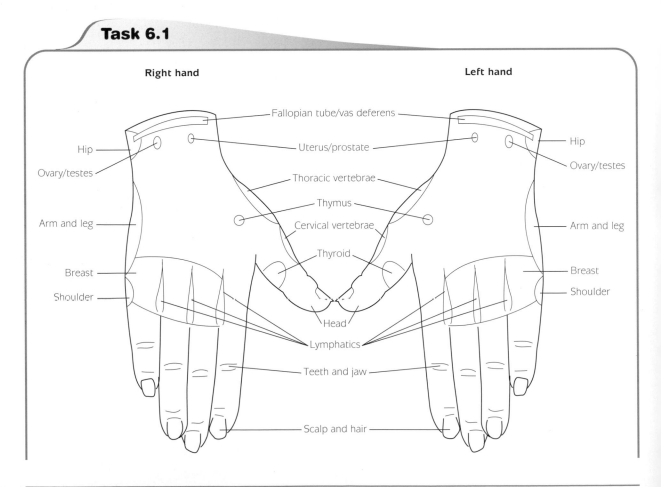

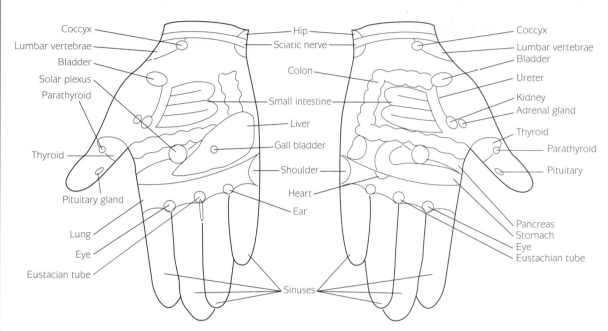

Figure 6.1 *Hand reflexology chart*

Locate the following reflexes and use a pencil to circle them on the chart.

Thyroid	Gall bladder
Small intestine	Bladder
Sciatic nerve	Eye
Lumbar vertebrae	Arm and leg
Pituitary gland	Ovaries and testes
Heart	

Uses of hand reflexology

Hand reflexology can be used instead of foot reflexology when:

- the foot is injured or there is an infection
- the foot has been amputated
- the client does not want their feet to be touched
- the patient is elderly and cannot lift their foot
- there is not enough time for a foot treatment.

As part of the homecare advice clients can be shown how to help themselves using hand reflexology.

Zones of the hands

The hands are split into zones in the same way as the feet.

Task 6.2

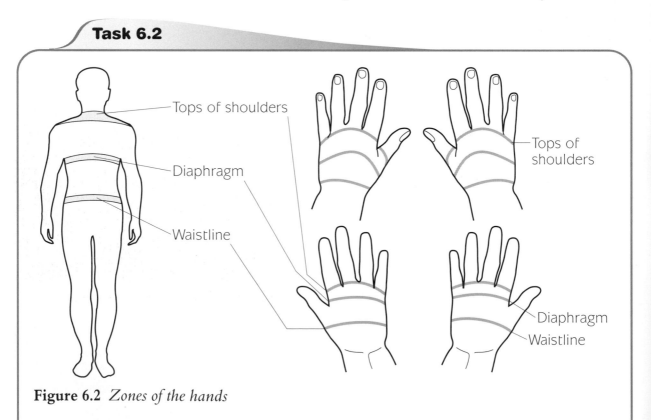

Tops of shoulders

Diaphragm

Waistline

Tops of shoulders

Diaphragm

Waistline

Figure 6.2 *Zones of the hands*

Find out where the following reflexes are and draw them on the chart on page 124.

Large intestine	Spine
Solar plexus	Shoulder
Heart	Stomach
Brain	Pancreas
Bladder	Liver
Parathyroids	Lymphatics
Fallopian tubes	

The hand reflexology treatment

The following sequence is not a complete hand reflexology routine. However, the diagrams will help you to locate certain reflexes on the hands. Start with the client's right hand; this will follow the natural direction of the colon as its reflex begins on the right hand and ends on the left hand.

1 **Rotation of the hand**
Hold the client's wrist, and with the other hand rotate the client's hand clockwise and then anticlockwise. Repeat four times each way.

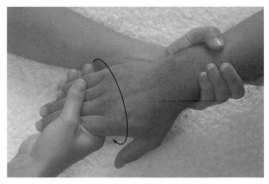

Figure 6.3 *Rotation of the hand*

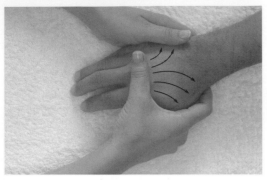

Figure 6.4 *Thumb stroke over top of hand*

2 **Thumb stroke over top of hand**
The thumbs are used to stroke over the top of the hand.

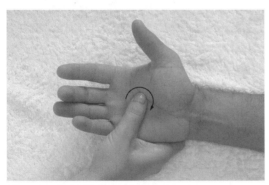

Figure 6.5 *Solar plexus*

3 **Solar plexus**
Turn the hand over so that the palm is facing upwards. If the hand is squeezed the solar plexus can be found in the depression just beneath the diaphragm. Use the thumb to press and rotate on the solar plexus.

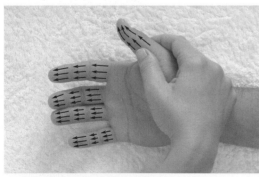

Figure 6.6 *Head/neck*

4 **Head/neck**
Use the thumb to work up and over all of the fingers, especially the thumb.

5 Pituitary/pineal and hypothalamus

The pituitary is found in the middle of the thumb. Use the thumb to press and rotate on the pituitary. Then press and rotate onto the medial side of the thumb to work the pineal and hypothalamus.

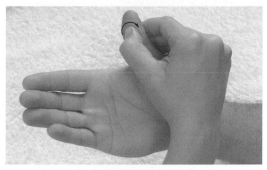

Figure 6.7a *Pituitary*

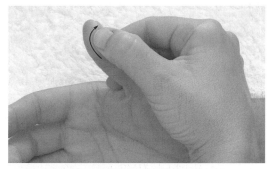

Figure 6.7b *Pineal and hypothalamus*

6 Sinuses

Thumb walk up the centre of each finger and then work up the sides. Slide your thumb up and over the fingers to help drain the sinuses.

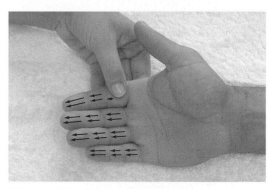

Figure 6.8 *Sinuses*

7 *Thyroid/parathyroid*

The thyroid reflex is found around the base of the thumb. Press and rotate onto the area.

The parathyroid reflex is found between the fingers (between zones 1 and 2). Press and rotate on this area.

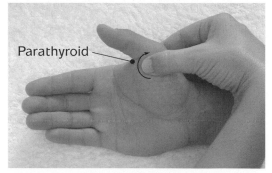

Parathyroid

Figure 6.9 *Thyroid/parathyroid*

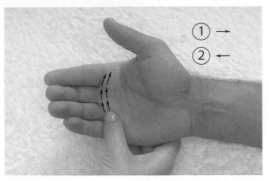

Figure 6.10 *Ears/eyes and eustachian tube*

8 *Ears/eyes and eustachian tube*
This reflex is found just below the base of the fingers. Thumb walk along this area and then change thumbs to work back the other way.

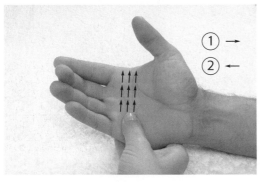

Figure 6.11 *Lung*

9 Lung
Thumb walk in rows over the chest area between zones 2 and 5. Work in another direction to ensure the area is covered thoroughly.

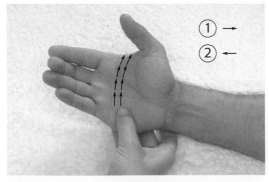

Figure 6.12 *Diaphragm*

10 Diaphragm
Thumb walk across the diaphragm line and back again.

11 Large intestine – ascending and transverse

The ascending colon is found between zones 4 and 5 on the right hand. Work up the colon towards and across the transverse colon.

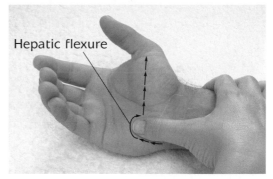

Figure 6.13 *Large intestine – ascending and transverse*

12 Small intestine

Found under the transverse colon between zones 4 and 1 on both hands. Thumb walk in rows across the small intestine.

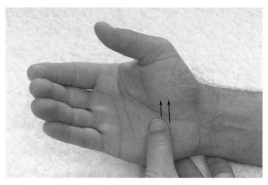

Figure 6.14 *Small intestine*

13 Liver and gall bladder

Found between zones 3 and 5 on the right hand. Thumb walk across the liver area in different directions to ensure it is covered thoroughly. Then press and rotate on the gall bladder.

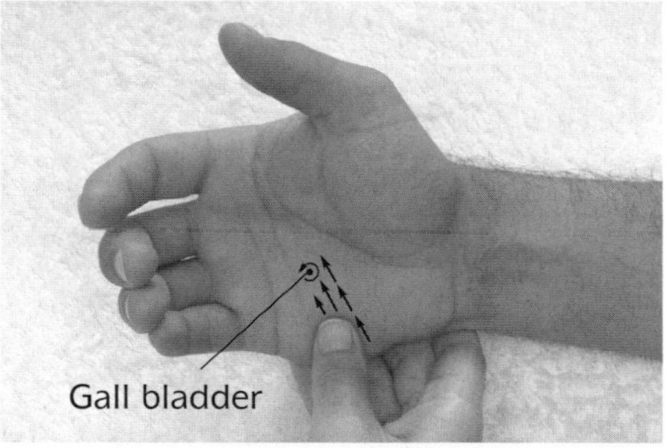

Figure 6.15 *Liver and gall bladder*

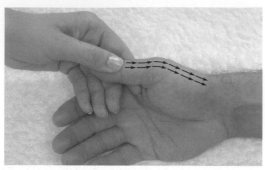

Figure 6.16 *Spine*

14 Spine
Found in zone 1 on each hand. Thumb walk from the thumb nail to the base of the palm, and then work back the other way.

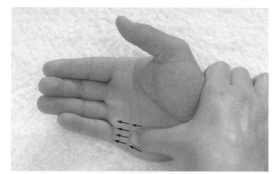

Figure 6.17 *Shoulder*

15 Shoulder
Found on the anterior and posterior sides of the hand in zones 4 and 5. Thumb walk over these areas.

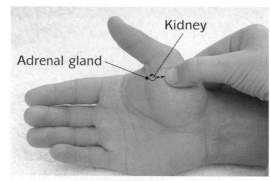

Figure 6.18a *Kidney/adrenal and ureter*

16 Kidney/adrenal/ureter and bladder
These organs are found in zones 1 and 2. Press and rotate on the kidney and adrenal gland and work across the ureter to the bladder. Thumb walk across the bladder.

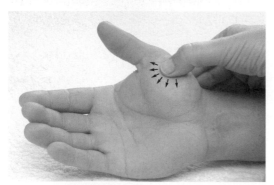

Figure 6.18b *Bladder*

17 Heart

Thumb walk across zones 3 and 4 in the area above the diaphragm and below the base of the fingers. The middle finger can be used to press the same area on top of the hand to create a linking movement and this will help increase energy flow.

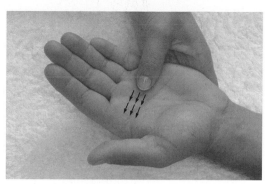

Figure 6.19 *Heart*

18 Pancreas/stomach

Found between zones 2 and 5 just below the diaphragm. Thumb walk over the area and back again.

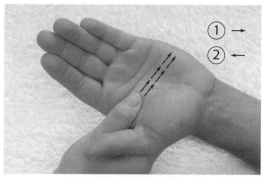

Figure 6.20 *Pancreas/stomach*

19 Transverse and descending colon

Found between zones 2 and 5 on the left hand. Thumb walk across the colon and rotate on the splenic flexure. Work down the descending colon and rotate on the sigmoid flexure. Continue thumb walking until you reach zone 1.

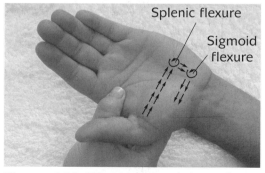

Figure 6.21 *Transverse and descending colon*

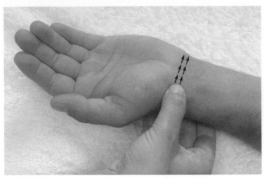

Figure 6.22 *Sciatic nerve*

20 Sciatic nerve

Found on the wrist between zones 1 and 5. Thumb walk across the area.

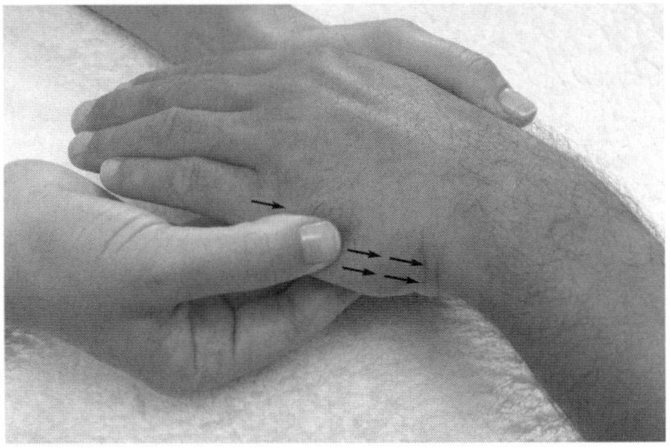

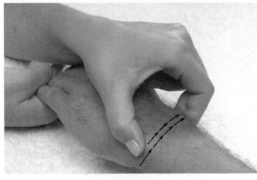

Figure 6.23 *Knee, hip and lower back*

21 Knee, hip and lower back

Found on the lateral side of the hand in zone 5. Thumb walk from the base of the little finger to the wrist.

22 Reproductive area

Place the thumb and finger on either side of the wrist and press. Thumb walk across the wrist to work the fallopian tubes and vas deferens.

Figure 6.24 *Reproductive area*

23 Breast/chest

Found between zones 3 and 5 on the back of the hand. Use the thumb to work over the area and back again.

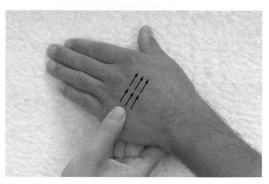

Figure 6.25 *Breast/chest*

24 Lymphatic

Found on all zones on the back of the hand. Finger walk along each zone and complete the treatment by stroking the thumbs or fingers over the same area in the direction of the wrist to help lymphatic drainage.

Complete the treatment by stroking the hands and pressing the solar plexus reflexes.

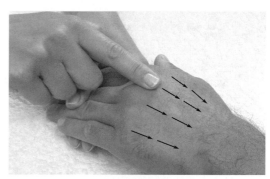

Figure 6.26a *Lymphatic (1)*

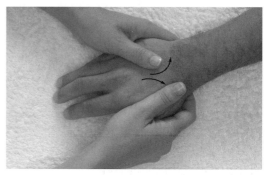

Figure 6.26b *Lymphatic (2)*

Auricular Therapy

Ear acupuncture has been practised for thousands of years and involves using needles to release energy. In the 1950s a French doctor called Paul Nogier introduced the theory that the ear corresponded to the inverted foetus. He found that areas of the body related to points found on the ear and he produced the first western map of the ear.

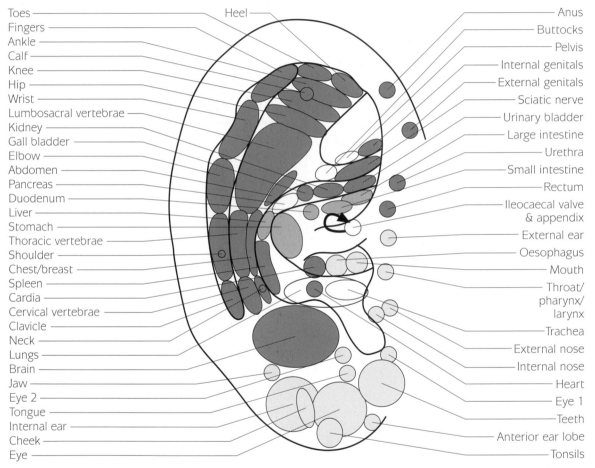

Figure 6.27 *The reflex points of the ear*

The finger and/or thumb can be used to apply pressure to certain areas of the ear to help treat specific conditions.

Interpreting the feet and giving client advice

7

If during treatment you come upon a tender spot and your client asks you what that represents or what implications for health that area has, your best answer is that it simply represents a region of the body (for example, the head section, pelvic area, abdominal area). You cannot tell them accurately that it represents a specific organ or gland because so many organs, muscles and glands overlap.

The reflexes will sometimes show imbalance when there is no actual physical problem. The energy of the area may be disturbed and might not be flowing freely; that could be caused by tension or physical or emotional trauma. Therefore there will be reflex imbalance that does not indicate a medical problem but is a warning sign of stress in that body part.

READING THE FEET

Carrying out a reflexology treatment is like being a detective and having to piece together all of the evidence. That is why the consultation is so important. For example, if a client informs you that she is suffering with headaches around the time of her period, would you just treat the head reflex area on the foot? No, you would also treat the endocrine glands, especially the pituitary and ovaries, because the information she has given indicates that the headaches may be related to hormonal factors. This approach is known as the holistic approach as we are taking into account the whole body when giving treatment.

You may sometimes be incorrect with your conclusions, but remember you are working the whole foot, so you will be covering all of the reflex areas during the treatment. The more practice and experience you gain, the better you will become at giving the reflexology treatment.

INDICATIONS AND SENSATIONS FELT DURING TREATMENT

While giving a reflexology treatment it is common to feel different sensations as you work over the feet. These include the following.

Crystals or grittiness that feel like sugar granules in the feet

Uric acid crystals and calcium deposits may have built up on the end of nerve endings and capillaries causing congestion. Working over this area with the thumbs and/or fingers will help to disperse these crystals and encourage energy flow and improved circulation in the corresponding body part.

Areas feeling hollow and empty

This could be due to poor energy flow, or sometimes it can be felt in areas where an organ has been removed, e.g. the uterus is removed when a hysterectomy is performed. If there is a build-up of scar tissue you may feel hardness in the corresponding area.

Popping and bubbling (similar to popping bubble wrap)

This could indicate an energy imbalance. It can commonly be felt in the large intestine and could be an indication of trapped wind in that area.

Hardness in reflex areas

This may indicate poor energy flow. It can sometimes be felt where there are areas of muscular tension and tightness. Working over these areas will help stimulate the circulation and thus increase oxygen and nutrient flow to the area, also aiding removal of toxins and so restoring energy flow.

Dampness

People who do not eliminate waste efficiently from the body may retain toxins. This will sometimes be the case if the feet are damp to the touch. Also make a note of the colour: if they are particularly yellow or orange in colour this may also signify poor elimination of waste. Another sign is if the feet smell like cheese.

Excessively sweaty feet

This may indicate a hormonal imbalance. It is advised to work on the endocrine system for hormonal balance. Other indications of hormonal imbalance include disturbed sleep patterns and irregular periods.

Temperature

Cold feet may indicate poor circulation and hot feet could be a sign of hormonal imbalance. Cold or hot feet (or specific areas of the feet) may also be a sign of energy imbalance in the body.

Colour

Blue or pale feet may indicate poor circulation and pink may show good circulation. If an area of the foot is very red it may be a sign that there is too much blood passing through the corresponding part of the body. This may mean that the flow of energy in this area needs balancing.

Smell

A cheesy smell could be a sign of poor detoxification so you will need to work the eliminatory channels such as the large intestine, kidneys and liver. It may also be smelt on people who eat too much animal and dairy food. An acetone smell could be linked to urinary problems and is also sometimes associated with someone suffering from diabetes. A musty smell may be due to a fungal infection of the nails.

Muscle tone

If the muscle tone in the feet is good, the muscle tone in the body is also good and vice versa.

Ingrowing toenail

The toenail will be growing into the head area and may be related to headaches and migraines.

Hard skin on reflex areas

Note

If a client is suffering with permanent heel cracks, has a yellow tint to the skin and very dry skin and hair it could indicate a thyroid imbalance.

Hard skin may be an indication that the body is trying to protect an area, e.g. a client may be suffering with sinusitis and hard skin is found on the tops of the toes. If a client is suffering with problems around the pelvic or lower back areas there may be dry, rough skin around the heel, which may be accompanied by cracks in the skin. Dry skin may be due to a lack of omega 3 and omega 6 essential fatty acids in the diet.

Bunions

A bunion on the big toe may indicate possible neck problems or hormonal imbalance. It may also be associated with headaches.

High or fallen arch

This condition will occur on the spinal reflexes, which could relate to back or spinal problems. Also make a note of the client's posture.

Hammer toes

As the toes are reflexes of the head and sinuses, hammer toes may be associated with headaches and migraines.

Tenderness/discomfort/pain

If during the treatment tenderness is experienced in a region of the foot, it may be linked to past trauma such as an operation or injury. Sometimes reflexes may not become tender until the third or fourth treatment as they lack sufficient energy to respond.

Watch the client's reaction to the treatment to see if they flinch, which will show that a reflex is painful. If the pain is sharp it may be a sign that the condition is acute. A dull pain may indicate a chronic condition.

If a client experiences a tingling sensation or warmth in the area of the body that is being worked on the foot, or elsewhere in the body (e.g. if whilst working the leg reflex on the foot the client feels a tingling sensation in their leg), it could indicate that energy has been unblocked and is therefore flowing more freely.

ENERGY IMBALANCE

If the client feels pain, sensitivity, grittiness etc. as you work the feet, these may all be indications that there could be energy imbalance in the body and this can be treated in the following ways:

- work slower and deeper over the affected area of the foot
- press and rotate over the area for a longer time
- work over the area many times
- return to the area again at the end of the treatment.

Clients can be shown hand reflexology to help their condition.

Use the information in this chapter to help you complete the table.

Table 7.1 Sensations felt during treatment

Sensation	Brief description of what the sensation may indicate
Crystals/grittiness	
Hollow empty area	
Popping and bubbling	
Hardness	
Dampness	
Excessively sweaty feet	
Temperature	
Colour	
Smell	
Muscle tone	
Ingrowing toenail	
Hard skin	
Bunions	
High or fallen arches	
Hammer toes	
Tenderness/pain	

Note

Flexible feet can indicate that the person is versatile and adapts easily and willingly to the ups and downs of life. If the feet are rigid it may mean that the person is harsh, strict, stubborn and set in their ways.

INTERPRETING NAIL COLOUR AND CONDITION

- White nail colour may be a sign of fungal growth or liver problems.

- White dots on the nails may indicate a zinc deficiency or slight injury to the nail.

- Brown nail colour may indicate fungal growth or kidney disease.

- Yellow nail colour could be due to jaundice, lung condition or of course too much smoking!

- Blue nails may indicate poor circulation or a heart or lung condition.

- Pitted nails may indicate a skin disorder such as psoriasis or eczema.

- Pale, brittle, ridged and concave nails may be a sign of anaemia.

- Breaking and splitting of nails may be a sign of thyroid problems.

- Nails that are half-white and half-pink may indicate a kidney disorder.

- Nails with a yellowish tint and pink colouring at the base of the nail may be linked to diabetes.

- Ridges on the nails may be linked to eczema or thyroid problems. Vertical ridges may indicate shock or trauma to the nail and horizontal ridges may be linked to a respiratory disorder.

- Curved nails may indicate a respiratory disorder.

Note

Never inform a client that, because of the condition of their nails, they may have kidney, heart or lung problems etc.!

FOOT ASSESSMENT CHART

The following chart may be used to help you record information discovered during the reflexology treatment. Letters and symbols etc. may be used to indicate areas of the feet that you would like to highlight on your chart e.g. 'g' could be written to indicate grittiness.

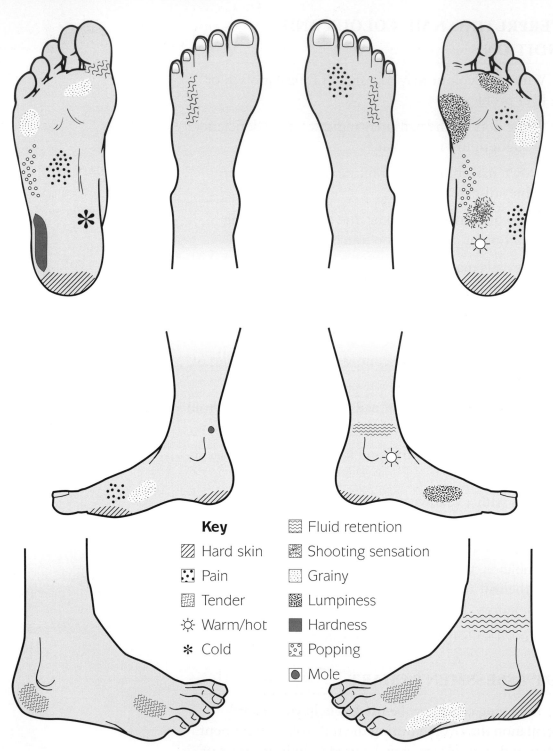

Key

▨	Hard skin	≈	Fluid retention
⋮	Pain	▨	Shooting sensation
▨	Tender	░	Grainy
☼	Warm/hot	▨	Lumpiness
✳	Cold	▮	Hardness
		⊡	Popping
		◉	Mole

Figure 7.1 *Example of foot chart completed during treatment*

Fill out your own foot assessment chart using the key on page 142 or make up your own.

AFTERCARE ADVICE

After the treatment the client may be given the following aftercare advice so that they gain maximum benefit from the reflexology. The aftercare advice should be followed for 24 hours.

- Rest and relax. Encourage the client to practise deep breathing and relaxation techniques. This will help ensure that the body is able to heal itself sufficiently.

- Drink some water to help flush out toxins from the body. This will also help to prevent contra-actions/healing crisis (see below).

- Eat only small meals. Eating large meals will cause blood to be diverted to the gut to help with the digestion of food. The demands of digestion will divert energy away from the healing processes. Light meals such as fruit and vegetables make ideal snacks.

- Avoid coffee, tea and cola as they contain caffeine. Caffeine is a stimulant and therefore will not help the client to relax.

- Do not smoke or drink alcohol for about 24 hours as the treatment is a detoxifying one and smoking and drinking will introduce toxins into the body.

You will need to adjust the aftercare advice so that it is relevant to each client. Maybe you feel the client needs to take regular exercise or you may want to recommend that they see another therapist, such as an aromatherapist, herbalist or nutritionist.

You could design a leaflet describing relaxation and breathing techniques. Advice regarding stress and how to deal with its negative effects may also be useful to the client.

Task 7.3

Study the information given on aftercare advice to enable you to answer the questions listed here.

1 Why should drinks containing caffeine be avoided after a treatment?

_____

2 Why should a client eat only light meals?

_____

3 Why should smoking and drinking alcohol be avoided after treatment?

_____

4 Why should water be drunk after treatment?

_____

5 Why should a client be advised to rest and relax after the treatment?

_____

ADVICE REGARDING HEALING CRISIS, ALSO KNOWN AS CONTRA-ACTION

After a reflexology treatment the client will usually feel relaxed, but occasionally a client may experience what is known as a 'healing crisis', although a more accurate description would be 'healing sign'. A healing crisis is a reaction that might occur during or after the reflexology treatment and could mean that the body is in the process of cleansing and healing itself. The healing process may also cause the client's symptoms to worsen for a while before they get better.

During treatment

◆ The release of toxins may cause tiredness, and the client may even fall asleep. The body will need to rest in order for its healing energies to carry out their work effectively.

◆ The client may feel a little emotional, perhaps even tearful. It is a good way for the client to release tension. They may laugh or talk a great deal too.

Other reactions that may occur during treatment include sweating, thirst, nausea or the need to pass water.

After treatment

Occasionally a client may report one or more of the following reactions up to 48 hours after treatment:

- headache
- nausea
- thirst
- they may develop a cold or sore throat
- sleepiness/fatigue
- vivid dreams
- frequent urination
- more frequent bowel movements
- increased mucus production such as in the nose
- sweating
- skin rash/breakout of spots
- aches and pains
- heavier menstrual flow
- symptoms are exacerbated.

Many of these reactions will be due to the flushing out of toxins and will soon settle down. They are also signs that the immune system is strengthened. Giving the client a glass of water after treatment will help the body to flush away these toxins.

If the client reports that they are suffering symptoms that are the opposite of this process of letting go, e.g. constipation, it is likely that it is not a healing crisis but something that was going to happen anyway.

Between treatments clients often report they have more energy, improved mood and relief of their symptoms.

Healing crisis reactions are short-lived and the client will feel a greater sense of well-being afterwards.

Note

Ensure you make a note on their record card of any of these reactions.

Dietary and exercise advice

Nutritional advice should only be given if the therapist has taken a professional course in nutrition. There is some general advice you may give to a client regarding lifestyle factors which include the following points:

- take 20 minutes of aerobic exercise, such as swimming or walking, at least three times a week

- eat five portions of fruit and/or vegetables every day to reduce the risk of cancer of the lung, breast, digestive tract, bladder and bowel

- drink two litres of water a day to flush the kidneys and to keep them healthy

- start the day with a glass of warm water and fresh lemon juice to stimulate the digestive system and eliminate toxins

- reduce salt as excessive intake is linked to high blood pressure, heart disease and kidney failure

- use olive oil as it is rich in monounsaturated fats which help prevent the oxidation of bad cholesterol (LDL) into its artery-clogging form

- drinking red wine (in moderation) can help raise levels of good cholesterol (HDL) and reduce the stickiness of blood as it contains a substance called resveratrol

- vegetarians may have a low intake of iron, calcium, zinc and vitamin B12, which are all found in meat. Advise them to eat egg yolks, fortified cereal and green leafy vegetables

- if the client smokes, advise them to increase their intake of antioxidant vitamins C and E as these help to counteract the effect of free radicals found in tobacco smoke that can cause cancer.

Research organisations such as RELATE, AA, The Samaritans, Age Concern etc. so that you have relevant information at hand if required by your client.

The following case studies, which relate to regular clients of the author, may be useful to you if you need to complete case studies as part of your course.

Case Study ➊

Case study name: Charlotte

Introduction/profile

Charlotte is 25 years old. She lives with her partner Zak and four-month-old son Ian. She is currently on maternity leave and has a job as a customer adviser. She is a non-smoker, drinks moderate amounts of alcohol, but does little exercise. She is happy with her life at present but is not looking forward to going back to her stressful job.

Presenting conditions and treatment plan

1) Headaches/stress: she regularly suffers with headaches. Reflexes to work include solar plexus, diaphragm, toes, neck, ears/eyes, adrenals, pituitary gland, hypothalamus and spine.
2) Sciatica: it bothers her mainly when she sits or stands for long periods of time. Reflexes to work include the spine, hip, pelvic area, buttocks and leg.

Medical history

- Blood pressure: she has low blood pressure, a problem for her during pregnancy due to fainting.
- Perspiration: she sweats excessively, unsure why. Could be a hormone imbalance.
- Headaches: she suffers headaches every other day; these started six or seven years ago. The pain is located above the eyes.
- Respiration: she occasionally suffers with asthma, blocked sinuses and produces a lot of mucus.
- Accidents: due to a car accident she suffered a broken wrist, elbow, finger and cracked eye socket.

Observations of the feet	◆ Colour: yellow in places, especially the toes and heels. ◆ Temperature: warm and clammy. ◆ Texture: smooth on dorsal surface and rough on plantar aspect, mainly shoulders and pelvic areas.
Therapist's findings	◆ Shoulders: congestion/grittiness in both feet. Zone 5 on the left foot and zone 4 on the right foot. ◆ Head: while working the big toe of the right foot she felt a tingling sensation at the back of her head. ◆ Toes: there was congestion over the sinus areas at the top of the toes of the right foot. She regularly suffers with blocked sinuses and excess mucus. ◆ Chest area: while working over the chest area of the right foot she had goose bumps and tingling in her leg. ◆ Breast/lymph: as I worked this area she felt a 'rush' over the back of her head. ◆ Large intestine: she felt a tingling sensation in her head while I worked this reflex on her left foot. ◆ Sacrum/coccyx: grittiness was found here. She suffers with lower back problems, probably due to an accident where she was thrown off a horse. ◆ Lung/chest: grittiness found on left foot.
Client's reaction to treatment/conclusion	Charlotte found the treatment relaxing. She was interested to know why she kept experiencing different sensations as I worked particular reflexes. I explained that was probably energy that may have been blocked and was now flowing freely in the body.

Second treatment

Introduction	Charlotte informs me that she no longer suffers with headaches. It happened directly after treatment, although she is unsure if this is due to the reflexology treatments or whether there is another reason that the headaches have stopped.
Presenting conditions and treatment plan	◆ Aching/clicking in hips: reflexes worked include hips, legs, spine. ◆ Tiredness: reflexes worked include the head, nervous system, endocrine glands, digestive system. I will work

the liver, large intestine and kidneys in case the tiredness is due to a build-up of toxins.

- Tension in shoulders: reflexes worked include shoulders, neck, arms, back, spine, head.

Observations of the feet

- Colour: pink, yellow callous skin on both big toes and in chest region, zones 2/3.
- Temperature: warm and clammy.
- Texture: smooth on dorsal aspect, rough on heels.

Therapist's findings

- Head reflex: calloused skin found on both big toes.
- Lung/chest reflexes: hard skin found in zone 2. She has no problems in this area at this time, although she suffers with asthma and sometimes excess mucus production.
- Shoulder reflex: grittiness found in left foot and also in zones 3 and 4 of right foot. She suffers with tension in her shoulders.
- Colon reflex: lumpiness was found in the ascending colon. She does not currently have problems in this region. Maybe there is a build-up of waste in this region.
- Pelvic area: congestion was found in this area of both feet. She is experiencing what she describes as 'twinges', although the discomfort has improved since the last treatment.

Client's reaction to treatment/conclusion

She found the treatments very effective. The headaches she often suffered have disappeared and she has had relief from the discomfort in her hips.

Case Study ❷   ## Case study name: Jayne

Introduction/profile

Jayne works as a customer service adviser for a bank. She feels her manager is putting a great deal of pressure on her and she often takes work home, for which she is not paid. She excels in her job but lacks confidence in her abilities despite winning awards for excellent service.

Jayne is in good health, although she was recently told she had slightly high blood pressure. However, the doctor was not concerned about this and thought it may be due to stressors such as the pressure at work and the fact that her husband was suffering ill health (heart problems). Jayne's sleep pattern is poor and she wakes early in the morning.

She leads a fairly healthy lifestyle, she does not drink a great deal of alcohol or smoke cigarettes. However, she is overweight and so her self-esteem is low.

Jayne has been going through the menopause for the last year, which has brought a host of symptoms including weight gain, bouts of anxiety, hot flushes and headaches.

Presenting conditions and treatment plan

Note

The pineal and adrenal glands control the sleeping and waking pattern.

1) High blood pressure: reflexes to work include the diaphragm/solar plexus, heart, lungs, liver, adrenal glands, kidneys, spinal nerves to these organs, and eliminative channels such as the large intestine.
2) Sleep problems: awakens at 4 a.m. every day; feels tired all day. Reflexes to work include pineal, hypothalamus and adrenal glands.
3) Menopause: endocrine glands, reproductive organs, spinal nerves, diaphragm, solar plexus.

Treatment

Orthodox medicine (advice and drugs given by doctor):
- High blood pressure: hypotensive drugs, cut down on salt intake, vegetarian diet, take more exercise.
- Menopause: hormone replacement therapy, special diet, exercise.
  I suggested that the following complementary therapy treatments may be beneficial to her conditions:
- High blood pressure: Bach flower remedies, yoga, tai chi, aromatherapy massage, use of essential oils.
- Sleep problems: Bach flower remedies, essential oils/massage, yoga or acupuncture.
- Menopause: essential oils/aromatherapy massage, Bach flower remedies, yoga, acupuncture, acupressure or herbalism.

Observation of the feet

- Colour: feet are very orange in colour, especially the balls and heels of the feet. I felt perhaps her liver was a little sluggish and was not detoxifying as well as it could resulting in orange-coloured feet.
- Temperature: clammy feet, very warm to the touch.

- Texture: soft and smooth to the touch. Calloused skin on chest region, zones 1 and 2 and around the heels.
- Blemishes: moles on chest area and on breast area (dorsal aspect).

Tender areas felt by client

- Neck reflex of right foot
- Pituitary gland of left big toe
- Ear/eye reflex – felt like sharp pin or nail (zone 3 and 4).

Therapist's findings

- Neck reflex of right foot and shoulders of both feet: grittiness.
- Large intestine (descending colon): bubbling.
- Sinus areas of second and third toes of left foot: grittiness.
- Lymphatic channels on dorsal aspect of right foot: grittiness.

Client's reaction to treatment

Jayne was not sure what to expect. Her feet were generally sensitive but responded well to the treatment. She found the treatment relaxing although, at times, a little painful. Jayne's body language seemed positive and I feel she enjoyed the treatment.

Second treatment

Jayne was delighted to tell me that since the treatment she has slept till 6 a.m. instead of 4 a.m. and as a result feels like she has more energy.

Jayne said she felt quite nauseous soon after the last treatment. I explained that this is known as a healing crisis (or healing achievement as I prefer to call it) and is probably a positive sign that the body is responding to treatment and so is detoxifying.

Conditions present and treatment plan

- Stress: work the diaphragm/solar plexus, pituitary and adrenal glands, kidneys.
- Menopause: work the endocrine glands, reproductive organs, spinal nerves, diaphragm, solar plexus.
- High blood pressure: reflexes to work include the diaphragm/solar plexus, heart, lungs, liver, adrenal glands, kidneys, spinal nerves to these organs, and eliminative channels.

Observation of feet	◆ Colour: orange and yellow. Definitely not as orange as in treatment one. ◆ Temperature: slightly clammy, warm. ◆ Texture: soft and smooth. Calloused skin on chest region, zones 1 and 2, also over the heels of both feet.
Therapist's findings	◆ Right big toe: grittiness around the top of the toe. ◆ Diaphragm: zone 3 felt hard. ◆ Solar plexus: was sensitive to the client. She is feeling a little stressed today. ◆ Shoulders: grittiness and lumpiness could be felt. She is probably holding tension in her shoulders. ◆ Large intestine: bubbling. ◆ Adrenal glands: she felt a sharp sensation as I worked them. Probably due to the release of too many stress hormones. ◆ Uterus on right foot: reflex felt very warm. Maybe there is too much energy here. I spent a little more time on this area to restore balance.

Note

The endocrine glands are often quite sensitive reflexes, which may cause a little discomfort to the client

Client's reaction to treatment/conclusions

Jayne said she felt wonderful the day after both treatments. Generally her energy levels have improved. She is delighted that she is sleeping more and it has helped her to cope with the stresses of daily life.

She has suffered with less anxiety and fewer hot flushes and headaches. (The headaches may have been linked to sleep deprivation.) She also feels that the advice I gave regarding drinking plenty of water has helped her a great deal.

Reflexology and medical conditions

8

If your client suffers with any of the following conditions, you can pay attention to certain reflexes during the reflexology treatment. The 'direct reflexes to work' column lists the most important areas to work during treatment, and the 'associated reflexes' are other areas that can be worked to help the condition.

Some of the conditions in the following table, such as pregnancy, are **contraindications** to treatment, so ensure that the advice of a doctor or midwife is sought prior to giving reflexology treatment. Be aware that according to some reflexology organisations some of the conditions mentioned are total contraindications, while others require caution to be exercised. See Chapter 2 for more information about contraindications.

> **Note**
>
> Work specific reflexes for between 30 and 60 seconds.

> **Note**
>
> Skin problems are often due to poor detoxification. Ensure the eliminatory channels, e.g. the kidneys, liver and lungs, are treated to help these conditions.

> **Note**
>
> If any medical condition first occurred during puberty, pregnancy or menopause (e.g. a skin condition may have occurred around the time of puberty), it may be hormone related so endocrine glands can be treated to help this condition.

Table 8.1 Medical conditions

Condition	Direct reflexes to work	Associated reflexes	Notes
Acne vulgaris and acne rosacea (caused by hormonal imbalance)	Reflex for affected area, e.g. the face	Thyroid, intestines, adrenal glands, ovaries/testes, pituitary gland, liver	The pituitary gland is worked as it controls the adrenal glands and ovaries and testes
Addiction to drugs/alcohol	Pituitary, pineal, hypothalamus, liver	Lymphatics, digestive system	Increasing serotonin levels from the brain may help to lift mood. Working the liver will help detoxify the body. Working the lymphatics will help cleanse and detoxify the immune system. A treatment should never be given to a person under the influence of drugs or alcohol
Adrenal gland disorders (such as Addison's disease and Cushing's syndrome)	Adrenal gland	Pituitary, thyroid, parathyroids, ovaries, testes, uterus or prostate	
Anaemia (caused by lack of iron and causes fatigue, dizziness, breathlessness)	Spleen, liver, kidneys	Lungs, digestive system	Kidneys produce hormones that stimulate the production of red blood cells. Spleen destroys old red blood cells and the iron will be used to make new red blood cells. The liver stores iron

Condition	Direct reflexes to work	Associated reflexes	Notes
Anorexia nervosa	Hypothalamus, pituitary glands, adrenal glands	Digestive system	Hypothalamus controls hunger. Adrenal gland hormones control nutrient levels in the blood
Anxiety (often linked to depression)	Adrenal glands, head, spine, heart, endocrine glands, solar plexus, diaphragm	Lungs, kidneys	Adrenal glands release hormones including cortisol and adrenalin in times of stress. Chinese philosophy says we store anxiety in our kidneys
Allergies	Work affected area, e.g. lungs; also work sinuses, immune system, endocrine, adrenal glands, digestive system	Spinal nerves, solar plexus, diaphragm	Often diet related. Hormones released from the adrenal cortex will help the body deal with allergies
Angina (a cramp in the heart muscle cue to lack of oxygen causing pain)	Heart	Solar plexus, diaphragm and adrenal glands. Shoulder and arm (if problems are experienced in these regions)	Working the solar plexus and diaphragm will help to relax and calm the client. Cortisol, released from the adrenal glands, is required to maintain the health and functioning of the heart and the cardiovascular system

Table 8.1 (continued)

Condition	Direct reflexes to work	Associated reflexes	Notes
Arthritis (inflammation, pain and stiffness in joints)	Affected area or cross reflex	Parathyroids, diaphragm, solar plexus, kidneys, spine, pituitary gland, adrenal glands, immune system	Immune system – arthritis is an autoimmune disorder whereby the body attacks its own tissues. Adrenal glands produce cortisol which helps reduce inflammation and pain
Arteriosclerosis (the artery walls harden and lose elasticity; this can lead to high blood pressure) Atherosclerosis (fatty deposits in the arteries)	Work the whole feet to help with these conditions. Also concentrate on the heart, adrenal glands, kidneys and thyroid		The kidneys release a hormone to help control blood pressure. Cortisol, released from the adrenals is needed to ensure the health and functioning of the heart and cardiovascular system
Asthma (walls of the air passage constrict so making breathing difficult)	Lungs, bronchi	Head, chest, solar plexus, diaphragm, cervical and thoracic spine, adrenals, ileo-caecal valve, pituitary, thyroid, heart	Working the bronchi reflexes will help to relax the bronchi and increase flow to the area. Working the thoracic spine will help nerve supply to the thoracic area. Working adrenals will help if asthma is caused by an allergy and will also help reduce inflammation. Adrenalin helps to open the air passages. Working the diaphragm helps to calm the whole body

Condition	Direct reflexes to work	Associated reflexes	Notes
Back pain	Spine, muscles around the spinal area, lower back	Kidneys, brain, sacroiliac joint, sciatic nerve, pelvic area, head, solar plexus	Working the spine will help relax muscles and relieve strain in this area. Working the brain may help to release endorphins. Cortisol from the kidneys will help with inflammation and pain. The kidneys may be the cause of the back pain
Bereavement	Solar plexus, diaphragm, pituitary, head, adrenal glands	Hypothalamus, pineal, stomach, spine, heart	Working the hypothalamus and pineal will help to treat tiredness and depression and balance the sleep pattern. Chinese philosophy says the stomach is the organ of sympathy and so weeps
Breast lumps (may be due to hormonal factors, cysts or fibrous tissue)	Breast	Lymphatic system, ovaries, pituitary, thyroid, adrenals	Ensure the client has sought medical help prior to reflexology treatment so that she is certain it is not breast cancer
Bronchitis (may be due to allergies or other factors and causes coughing and wheezing)	Lungs, bronchi	Solar plexus, diaphragm, adrenal glands, ileo-caecal valve	Cortisol helps to reduce inflammation

Table 8.1 (continued)

Condition	Direct reflexes to work	Associated reflexes	Notes
Bursitis, e.g. tennis elbow (inflammation of sacs surrounding joints)	Work the relevant joint and the lumbar spine for the knee and the cervical spine for the elbow	Referral area, adrenal glands	Working the nerves of the spine will help the affected nerve supply to the part. Adrenal glands releaseanti-inflammatory hormones
Chronic Fatigue Syndrome (M.E.) (may be due to a virus, causes flu-like symptoms, e.g. tiredness and weakness)	Pituitary, immune system, liver, spine, solar plexus, hypothalamus/pineal	Diaphragm, thymus, digestive system, spleen, lymphatic system, thyroid	A virus may cause this condition so working the immune system will help. Thyroid hormones help to control how energetic a person is. Treating the hypothalamus and pineal will help increase energy levels and relieve depression
Cirrhosis of the liver (often due to excess alcohol consumption)	Liver	Pancreas, eyes, all endocrine glands	In Chinese medicine the eyes are associated with the liver
Colds	Lymphatic system, respiratory system, sinuses, immune system, diaphragm, chest, throat, head	Digestive system	Do not treat if the client has a very high temperature. Working the lymphatic system will help fight infection and remove toxins. Working the sinuses will help to relieve congestion and assist in mucus drainage
Colitis (inflammation of the colon causing cramping pain)	Large intestine (also known as colon and bowel)	Solar plexus, adrenal glands, liver, gall bladder	

Condition	Direct reflexes to work	Associated reflexes	Notes
Constipation (this condition may cause toxins to build up and then pass out through the intestine wall to join the blood stream and lead to health problems such as headaches and skin conditions)	Large intestine	Liver, gall bladder, small intestine, ileo-caecal valve, diaphragm, lumbar spinal nerves, solar plexus, adrenal glands	Advise client to eat foods containing fibre such as fresh vegetables, fruit, whole cereals and legumes, which all have different cleansing effects on the body and so help detoxification. Working the colon reflex will help with the removal of waste. Working the gall bladder with help stimulate bile, which is a mild laxative, and lubricate the intestines
Cramps (may be due to build-up of waste in muscle, or lack of salt, or fatigue or poor blood circulation)	Work affected area, adrenal glands, spine, kidneys, parathyroid	Diaphragm, lungs, referral area if required	Parathyroid hormones controls calcium levels in the blood – calcium is needed for muscle contraction. The kidneys filter waste from the blood. Adrenal hormones control the balance of salt and potassium in the body. Potassium is needed for muscle contraction
Cystitis (due to bacterial infection)	Bladder, kidneys and ureters	Immune system, adrenal glands, lumbar spine and coccyx, lymphatic system, pelvic area, solar plexus	Adrenal glands release anti-inflammatory substances

Table 8.1 (continued)

Condition	Direct reflexes to work	Associated reflexes	Notes
Depression	Endocrine glands especially pituitary and pineal, head/brain, diaphragm, solar plexus	Liver, digestive system, heart	Brain – will help release mood-lifting endorphins and help raise serotonin levels to combat depression. In Chinese medicine the heart is associated with the emotion of joy, so working this reflex will help with conditions such as depression
Diabetes mellitus (due to insufficient insulin levels)	Pancreas	Liver, kidneys, adrenals, digestive system, pituitary gland, eyes	Pancreas – will help balance levels of hormones released from this gland. Adrenal hormones control nutrient (sugar) levels in the blood. Be aware that the skin may be thin so could be damaged, and also healing is poor. Research shows that reflexology treatment disturbs the sugar/insulin levels for a couple of hours immediately afterwards
Diarrhoea (may cause nutrients and fluid to be lost from the body)	Colon	Liver, adrenal glands, solar plexus	May be caused by virus/bacteria or stress, so work the appropriate reflexes. The client needs to ensure they have sufficient intake of fluids. If diarrhoea is due to lactose intolerance the client should avoid milk

Condition	Direct reflexes to work	Associated reflexes	Notes
Diverticulitis (sac-like pouches in the wall of the colon that become inflamed. May lead to narrowing of the intestinal wall)	Colon, small intestine	Liver, gall bladder, adrenals, diaphragm, solar plexus, lower spine, small intestine	Adrenal hormones, cortisol, will help to reduce inflammation. Working the colon will help to strengthen the muscular walls of the colon and increase blood circulation to the area to aid healing. The gall bladder releases bile, which is a mild laxative
Ear conditions (such as infections)	Ears, eustachian tube	Lymphatic, cervical spine, sinuses, solar plexus, adrenal glands	Eustachian tube – in case there is an infection that has passed from this tube to the middle ear
Eczema/dermatitis (dry, reddened, itchy, inflamed skin. Due to many factors such as allergies or stress)	Affected area	All endocrine glands especially adrenals, diaphragm, solar plexus, digestive system, liver, kidneys, lungs	Condition may be stress induced, or as a result of eating certain foods. Adrenal glands release anti-inflammatory and anti-allergenic substances. Chinese theory says that the skin and lungs are linked, e.g. eczema is often linked to asthma
Emphysema (Damage to alveoli in lungs. May be due to smoking and causes breathlessness)	Lungs, bronchi	Solar plexus, diaphragm, adrenal glands, ileo-caecal valve, lymphatic system	

Table 8.1 (continued)

Condition	Direct reflexes to work	Associated reflexes	Notes
Endometriosis (pieces of the endometrium form in the fallopian tubes, ovaries, bladder, intestines etc. causing irritation to surrounding tissue and painful periods)	Reproductive and endocrine system, pituitary and adrenal glands	Spinal nerves	Reproductive and endocrine systems help to restore hormonal balance
Eye disorders (e.g. infection)	Eye	Head, face, all toes, neck, spinal nerves, lymphatic system	
Flatulence (excessive gas production)	Small intestine, ileo-caecal valve, stomach	Liver, gall bladder, pancreas	
Fluid retention (oedema). (May occur due to hormonal changes or if the heart or kidneys are functioning poorly)	Heart, kidneys, lymphatic system	Urinary system, all endocrine glands, lumbar spine, area affected, pituitary gland	Heart – to improve circulation; pituitary gland as it releases anti-diuretic hormones. Kidneys control fluid levels in the body. Over-secretion of aldosterone from the adrenal glands causes increased levels of salt in the body, which leads to fluid retention. Lymphatic system drains excess tissue fluid. If treatment can be given, it might be necessary to use gentle pressure as the skin and feet may be vulnerable due to the swelling

Condition	Direct reflexes to work	Associated reflexes	Notes
Food allergies	Digestive tract	Adrenal glands, solar plexus, spleen	The client should be advised to seek help to discover the cause of the allergy
Fungal infections	Area affected (as long as the fungal infection is not on an area directly worked over), immune system	Adrenal glands	Cortisol helps to reduce inflammation
Gall stones (substances found in bile such as calcium and cholesterol can become solid and form gall stones)	Liver, gall bladder	Thyroid, parathyroid, solar plexus	Constipation may be a sign of poor gall bladder function or stones, as bile that is released from the gall bladder helps to move food through the intestines
Glandular fever (caused by a virus, symptoms include fever, swollen lymph glands and sore throat)	Lymphatic system, general reflexology treatment	Digestive system	Lymphatic system helps to produce white blood cells to fight infection. An efficient digestive system will ensure nutrients are being absorbed to help the body deal with infection
Goitre (swelling of the thyroid and may be due to lack of iodine in the diet)	Thyroid	Pituitary, adrenal glands	Pituitary controls the thyroid gland

Table 8.1 (continued)

Condition	Direct reflexes to work	Associated reflexes	Notes
Gout (due to build-up of uric acid in the blood. Pain, swelling and redness will be found at a joint)	Reflexes to affected area and referral area	Kidneys, large intestines, liver, all endocrine glands	Kidneys, liver and large intestines help to eliminate waste. Adrenal hormones help with inflammation
HIV/AIDS (caused by a virus and can be spread via infected blood)	Lymphatic system, general reflexology treatment	Head/brain, solar plexus, diaphragm	Risk is small if there are no open cuts or wounds on the skin. Reflexologist may wear disposable gloves
Haemorrhoids, aka piles (dilated blood vessels inside or outside the anus)	Rectum	Large intestine, solar plexus, adrenal glands	Cortisol is needed to maintain the functioning of the cardiovascular system
Hay fever (an allergic reaction that results in redness, sneezing, swelling, itching and the production of excess mucus)	Sinuses, head, face, eyes	Adrenal glands, throat, respiratory organs, diaphragm, ileo-caecal valve, lymphatic system, lungs, spleen, solar plexus	Hormones from the adrenal glands can help the body deal with allergies

Condition	Direct reflexes to work	Associated reflexes	Notes
Headache (stress and tension is the most common cause of headaches)	Head, neck	Shoulders, endocrine glands, digestive system, liver and kidney, face, sinuses, eyes, solar plexus, cervical spine, pituitary, thyroid, adrenals, ovaries	Headaches may be linked to irritable bowel syndrome, constipation, sluggish liver, dietary factors and hormonal imbalances. Toxin build-up in the colon may cause occipital headaches. May also be due to poor hydration so fluid intake (especially water) needs to be increased. If the headache persists for more than three days the client should consult their doctor
Hepatitis (infection and inflammation of the liver)	Liver	Lymphatic system, spleen, gall bladder	
Hernia (hiatus) (upper part of stomach pushes through the opening in the diaphragm)	Stomach	Spinal nerves, oesophagus, adrenals, diaphragm, solar plexus	This condition is more common in those who are overweight, smoke and have physically demanding occupations

Table 8.1 (continued)

Condition	Direct reflexes to work	Associated reflexes	Notes
High blood pressure and low blood pressure	Heart	Diaphragm, solar plexus, heart, liver, kidneys, spinal nerves, pituitary, thyroid, head/brain, adrenal glands	For low blood pressure it is advised to work more on the adrenal glands as these hormones increase blood pressure. Cortisol, released from the adrenal glands, is needed to ensure the health and functioning of the cardiovascular system. The thyroid affects the metabolism, which has an effect on the heart rate. The kidneys release a substance called renin, which helps regulate the blood pressure
Impotence (mostly caused by insufficient release of nitric oxide, which relaxes the walls of the arteries in the penis)	Testes, prostate, all glands, lower spine	Solar plexus, diaphragm, head	Other causes include anxiety, depression and diabetes. The drug Viagra is used to help this condition
Incontinence (often due to weakened bladder muscles, e.g. after childbirth)	Bladder, kidneys, ureters	Pelvic area, lumbar spine, coccyx, adrenal glands, prostate	Kidneys and adrenal glands control the amount of fluid in the body. Incontinence can be a sign of cystitis, kidney disease and prostate problems
Indigestion (discomfort in the chest area, often after eating)	Stomach, oesophagus	Digestive system including liver and gall bladder, diaphragm, solar plexus, adrenal glands	Client should be encouraged to chew food slowly as this may be a factor causing indigestion

Condition	Direct reflexes to work	Associated reflexes	Notes
Infertility	Reproductive organs	Pituitary, thyroid, adrenal glands, solar plexus, diaphragm, lower spine, immune system	The pituitary gland has a controlling effect on the ovaries. A poor diet, stress and excess body weight can also decrease chances of becoming pregnant. If possible treat both partners
Insomnia (disturbed sleep or inability to get to sleep may be due to dietary factors or stress)	Head/brain, solar plexus, diaphragm, spine, endocrine glands especially adrenal glands	Hypothalamus, pineal gland	Pineal gland releases melatonin to control sleep/wake pattern. Serotonin is released from the brain and is thought to help promote sleep. Adrenal cortex hormones and hypothalamus also control sleep/wake patterns. Working the diaphragm and solar plexus will help to relax the client
Irritable bowel syndrome (symptoms include abdominal pain and alternating diarrhoea and constipation)	Large intestine, small intestine	Ileo-caecal valve, solar plexus, diaphragm, adrenals, liver, gall bladder, pancreas, lower spine	May be stress induced, so work on reflexes that help the client to relax
Kidney stones (due to a build-up of calcium and other salts in one or both kidneys)	Bladder, kidneys, ureters	Adrenal glands, diaphragm, solar plexus, parathyroids	May be associated with gout, kidney or parathyroid problems. Parathormone from the parathyroids help to control calcium levels in the body. Mineral corticoids (aldosterone) help control the balance of salt in the body

Table 8.1 (continued)

Condition	Direct reflexes to work	Associated reflexes	Notes
Knee problems	Knee	Leg, hip, sciatic, spinal nerves, pelvic area, referral area	The cross-reflex to the knee is the elbow
Labour pains	Uterus	Spinal nerves/muscles, pituitary gland, brain, adrenal glands, diaphragm, solar plexus	Oxytocin from the pituitary gland controls the contractions
Leg problems	Leg	Hip, knee, spinal nerves, referral area	The cross-reflex to the leg is the arm
Leukaemia (cancer of the blood due to over-production of white blood cells)	Lymphatic system especially the spleen	All endocrine glands, digestive system, liver, kidneys, lungs	Medical advice must be sought prior to treatment. The liver stores and filters the blood
Menopausal problems (symptoms include hot flushes, headaches, depression and dry skin/hair)	Endocrine glands, reproductive system, head, spinal nerves, liver, chronic uterus area	Diaphragm and solar plexus	After menopause, oestrogen levels drop causing an increase in parathyroid hormones, so excess calcium is taken from the bones leading to osteoporosis. Serotonin, released from the brain, is thought to help control temperature in the body so may help with hot flushes. The hypothalamus also controls the body temperature

Condition	Direct reflexes to work	Associated reflexes	Notes
Menstruation problems	Ovaries, fallopian tubes, uterus, spinal nerves, pituitary gland	Lumbar spine and coccyx	Pituitary gland has a controlling effect on the ovaries
Multiple sclerosis (break down of myelin sheath and may cause muscular weakness, problems with speech and eyesight, and loss of coorcination)	Head, brain, spine	Adrenal glands, solar plexus, reflex for affected area, eyes, bladder and large intestine	
Migraine	Head, neck	All toes, pituitary, spine, neck, liver, diaphragm, solar plexus, intestines	May be stress induced, hormone related or due to sensitivity to food. Could be related to the digestive system or liver
Neck problems/pain	Neck	Shoulders, head, spine, all toes	Tension in the neck, leads to tension in the scalp and can cause headaches
Nephritis or Bright's disease (inflammation of the kidney)	Bladder, ureter, kidneys	Lymphatic system, pelvic area, adrenal glands, solar plexus	

Table 8.1 (continued)

Condition	Direct reflexes to work	Associated reflexes	Notes
Parkinson's disease (a disease that affects the brain and causes tremors, weakness and muscle stiffness)	Head, brain	Spine, diaphragm, solar plexus, adrenal glands	
Pelvic inflammatory disease (bacterial infection of reproductive organs)	Reproductive system	Pituitary glands, adrenal glands, lymphatic system	
Pleurisy (inflammation of the pleural lining of the lungs)	Lungs, bronchi	Solar plexus, diaphragm, adrenal glands, lymphatic system	
Pneumonia (inflammation of the lungs due to infection)	Lungs, bronchi	Solar plexus, diaphragm, adrenal glands, spleen, lymphatic system	
Pregnancy	Reproductive system	All endocrine glands, solar plexus, diaphragm, spine, bladder	Reflexology is not recommended in the first trimester (i.e. the first three months). Remember: pregnancy can lead to conditions such as high blood pressure and varicose veins. A study has shown that women receiving reflexology throughout pregnancy have a shorter and more comfortable labour

Condition	Direct reflexes to work	Associated reflexes	Notes
Pre-menstrual syndrome	All endocrine glands	Head, hypothalamus, diaphragm, solar plexus, kidneys, lymphatic system	Serotonin (which is released from the brain) and the hypothalamus are thought to help control moods
Prostate problems	Prostate, chronic prostate area	All endocrine glands, bladder, lower spine	Enlargement of the prostate is common in middle-aged men
Psoriasis (dry, inflamed reddened skin)	Affected area	Liver, kidneys, large intestines, small intestine, pituitary glands, adrenal glands, solar plexus, lungs	May be linked to sluggish liver and poor elimination of waste. The adrenal glands release cortisol, an anti-inflammatory hormone. Chinese theory says that the skin and lungs are linked
Sciatica (pain in lower back, through buttock and down leg)	Sciatic area, chronic sciatic area	Lumbar spine, coccyx, leg, pelvic/hip	Often due to pressure from the vertebral discs on the spinal nerves
Shingles (herpes zoster)	Reflexes on foot that relate to the affected areas on the body	Lymphatic system, spleen, solar plexus, brain/head, adrenal glands, immune system	Adrenal glands to help with inflammation and pain. Head/brain to help treat the pain
Sinusitis (inflammation of the membranes that line the sinuses thus causing pain)	Sinuses, ear/eye, head, facial area, adrenal glands	Ileo-caecal valve, adrenal glands, lymphatic system, cervical spine	Working the sinuses will he p to relieve congestion. Adrenals release hormones that help reduce inflammation and relieve pain. Working the ileo-caecal valve will help normalise mucus production

Table 8.1 (continued)

Condition	Direct reflexes to work	Associated reflexes	Notes
Stress/tension	Head, brain, diaphragm, solar plexus, spine, endocrine glands	Digestive system	The digestive system is often affected when we are stressed, and absorption of nutrients is highly important at this time
Stroke (cerebral haemorrhage or a clot that can cause paralysis)	Head, spine, brain, areas of body affected by the stroke	Heart, adrenal glands, solar plexus	Cortisol, released from the adrenal glands, helps to maintain the health and functioning of the cardiovascular system. GP advice is definitely required because treatment soon after a stroke may exacerbate bleeding or dislodge a clot and cause a further stroke
Throat infection	Throat	Neck, upper lymphatics, adrenal glands	Cortisol from the adrenal glands will help reduce inflammation and pain
Thyroid problems (thyroid can be under-active or over-active)	Thyroid	Pituitary, neck	The pituitary controls the thyroid. Iodine, which is needed to produce its hormones, is obtained from the food we eat
Tinnitus (ringing in the ears. Causes include ear disorder, injury and stress)	Ear, eustachian tube, brain, sinuses	Neck, kidneys, solar plexus, diaphragm	According to Chinese medicine, the ears are linked to the kidneys
Tonsillitis (inflammation of the tonsils)	Throat, sinuses, neck	Cervical spine, thymus gland, all toes, lymphatic system, adrenals, immune system	Hormones from the adrenal glands help with inflammation

Condition	Direct reflexes to work	Associated reflexes	Notes
Tiredness	Hypothalamus/pineal, pituitary	Spine, thyroid, adrenal glands, digestive system especially large intestine, liver, kidney, head	Hormones from the thyroid help control our energy levels. A build-up of toxins in the body will cause tiredness. Poor diet or sensitivity to certain foods can often make a person feel tired. Working the hypothalamus and pineal with help increase energy levels and relieve depression. Cortisol from the adrenal glands helps to control sleep and waking patterns, as does the hypothalamus
Ulcers (peptic and duodenal)	Stomach, duodenum	Solar plexus, diaphragm, adrenal glands	
Urethritis (spread of cystitis infection to the urethra)	Bladder, kidneys, ureters	Lymphatic system, adrenal glands, solar plexus, pelvic area	
Varicose veins (often blue in colour, and mainly due to the valves in the veins not functioning properly)	Reflex for affected area, heart	Referral area, adrenal glands	Never work directly over a varicose vein. Working the heart reflex will help stimulate blood circulation. Cortisol, released from the adrenal glands, is needed for the health and functioning of the heart and cardiovascular system

Other complementary therapies

9

REFLEXOLOGY AND MERIDIANS

In reflexology the foot can be divided into zones; in acupuncture the lines are known as meridians and carry vital energy. The Chinese discovered that energy, called Chi, circulates along the 12 meridian channels in the body. Six of the main meridians, that pass through the major organs in the body, are found in the feet (especially in the toes) and these include the liver, spleen/pancreas, stomach, gall bladder, bladder and kidney meridians. Reflexology helps to clear blockages along the meridians and encourages energy to flow so that the body is able to achieve a state of balance.

If the condition you are treating does not get better by working the specific reflex areas, you can treat the reflex area of the organ related to that meridian. For instance:

- If the client is experiencing pain in the lower back, work the bladder reflex area as the bladder meridian passes through the lower back.

- If there is an energy blockage in the stomach meridian it may cause toothache as this meridian passes through the upper gums, so you can work over the stomach reflex area to help treat toothache.

- The meridian for the small intestine runs through the arm, so if the client is experiencing a problem in the arm area, it may be caused or made worse due to a disorder of the small intestine. You could work the small intestine reflex area on the foot to help this problem.

- The bladder meridian passes through the head. If headaches occur check if the client has a history of bladder problems.

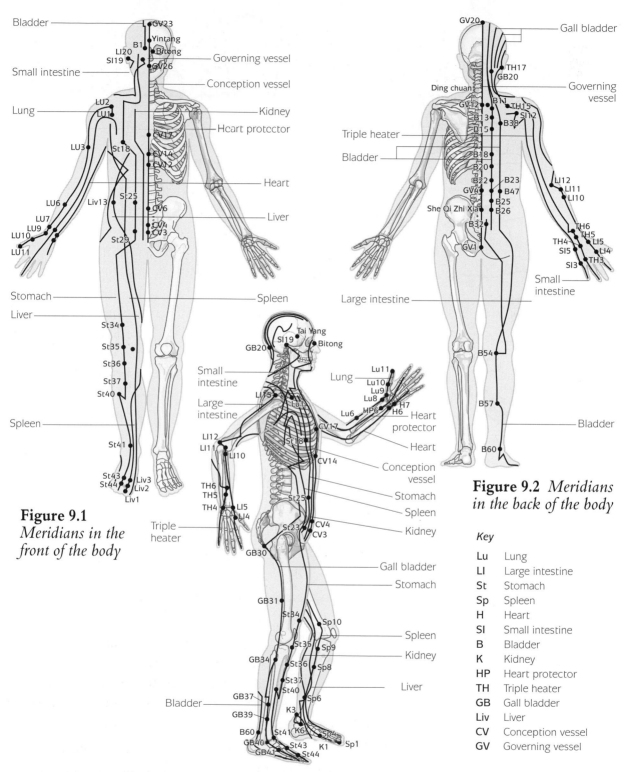

Figure 9.1 *Meridians in the front of the body*

Figure 9.2 *Meridians in the back of the body*

Figure 9.3 *Meridians in the side of the body*

Key

Lu	Lung
LI	Large intestine
St	Stomach
Sp	Spleen
H	Heart
SI	Small intestine
B	Bladder
K	Kidney
HP	Heart protector
TH	Triple heater
GB	Gall bladder
Liv	Liver
CV	Conception vessel
GV	Governing vessel

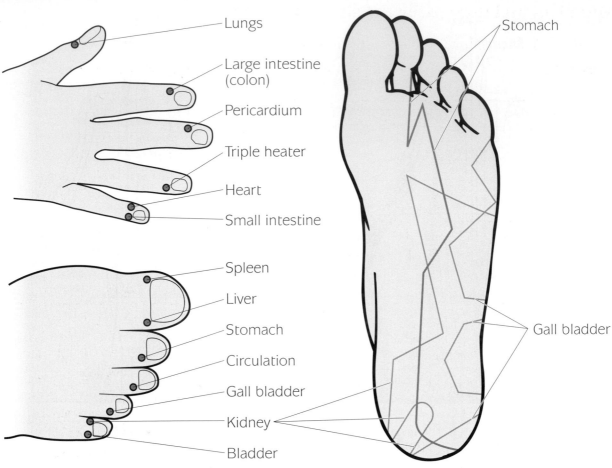

Figure 9.4 *Meridians in the feet and hands*

Working on the meridians shown will help to stimulate energy flow through them.

Task 9.1

On the meridian diagrams, colour each meridian as follows:

- stomach (yellow)
- spleen/pancreas (dark green)
- kidney (light blue)
- bladder (orange)
- gall bladder (red)
- liver (pink)

- lung (purple)
- large intestine (brown)
- small intestine (grey)
- heart (dark blue)
- circulation (light green).

Meridians and their pathway through the body

Table 9.1 Meridians and their pathway through the body

Meridian	Body parts and organs that the meridian passes through
Stomach	Begins under the eye, curves up to the temple and then down the body and ends on the top of the second toe. Areas of the body it passes through include the sinuses, throat, lungs, diaphragm, spleen, liver, gall bladder, stomach, pancreas, duodenum, adrenal glands, kidneys, large intestine, small intestine and pelvic region
Spleen/pancreas	Begins at the tip of the big toe, runs up the leg, over the pelvis, up the side of the abdomen and ends at the shoulder. Areas of the body it passes through include the throat, thyroid, underarm, digestion, pelvis, thigh, knee and skin
Kidney	Starts on the sole of the foot and flows up the back of the leg, around the front of the lower thigh and up the body to the breast bone. Areas of body it passes include the throat, lungs, heart, breast, solar plexus, diaphragm, groin, leg, uterus/prostate and bladder
Bladder	Begins at the inner corner of the eye, runs over the crown of the head, down the back of the legs and ends on the outer side of the back of the little toe. Areas of the body it passes through include the brain, spinal cord and nerves and indirectly it affects all of the body's organs
Gall bladder	Begins at the outer corner of the eye, runs across the temple, over the shoulder, continues down the leg and ends on the back of the fourth toe
Liver	Begins at the back of the big toe and runs up the leg to the groin and up to just below the nipple
Lung	Starts at the collar bone and ends at the back of the thumb on the side nearest the index finger
Large intestine	Starts from the tip of the index finger, crosses the back of the shoulder and ends at either side of the nose
Small intestine	Starts on the outside tip of the little finger and passes up along the back of the forearm. It passes behind the shoulder, along the side of the neck to the cheek and outer corner of the eye then enters the ear

Table 9.1 (continued)

Meridian	Body parts and organs that the meridian passes through
Heart	Begins under the arm and ends at the back of the little finger
Circulation/ pericardium	Flows from the nipple, down the arm and ends on the back of the middle finger
Triple burner	Begins on the back of the third finger, runs up the arm and ends at the top of the outer corner of the eye

Note

The stomach meridian is the main meridian as it passes through all major organs and is often the major cause of congestion.

Note

When working the feet during reflexology treatment you will be stimulating energy flow through the meridians.

ACUPRESSURE

The fingers and thumbs are used on specific points of the body to either strengthen, disperse or calm the Qi or Chi (energy) to help it flow smoothly in order to bring a balance between body and mind, relieving any symptoms.

Note

Do not use acupressure techniques on pregnant women.

Acupressure points can be found on areas of depressions where, for instance, there are indents in the bones. Pressure is used on each acupoint for between 30 seconds and two minutes.

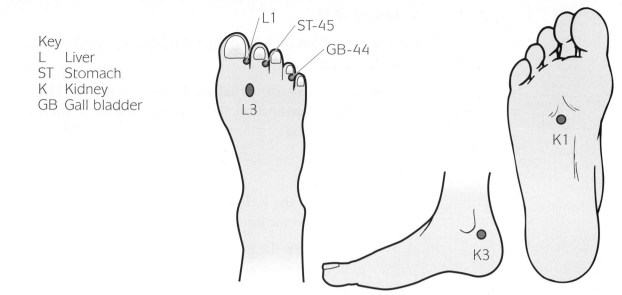

Figure 9.5a *Acupressure points on the feet*

Feet

Examples of acupressure points found on the feet include the following.

Kidney 1 (K1)

- Found in the same position as solar plexus reflex, just below the diaphragm.

- Helps to re-energise the body and relieve fatigue. Helps to balance blood pressure. Clears the mind, improves memory and concentration. Useful for anxiety conditions.

Kidney 3 (K3)

- Found on the inside of the ankle between the ankle bone and the Achilles tendon.

- Improves circulation in the feet and lower body. Improves kidney and heart functions.

Liver 1 (L1)

♦ Found on the lateral side of the big toe at the base of the nail.

♦ Relieves all menstrual and bladder problems. Helps relieve constipation and discomfort in the lumbar area of the spine.

Liver 3 (L3)

♦ Found on the web between the first and second toes, just before the join of the metatarsals and phalanges.

♦ Strengthens the liver and aids detoxification. Helps to relieve depression.

Stomach 45 (ST–45)

♦ Found on the lateral side of the second toe at the base of the nail.

♦ Helpful for mouth problems including tonsillitis and toothache.

Gall bladder 44 (GB–44)

♦ Found on the lateral side of the fourth toe at the base of the nail.

♦ Helps to alleviate headaches and any other problem relating to the ears, eyes and mouth. Also aids breast and lungs problems.

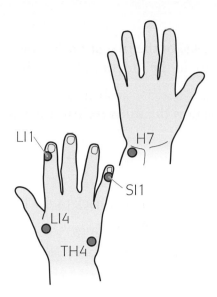

Key
LI   Large intestine
H   Heart
SI   Small intestines
TH   Triple heater

Figure 9.5b *Acupressure points on the hands*

Hands

Examples of acupressure points found on the hands include the following.

Large intestine 1 (LI1)

- Found at the base of the nail on the index finger, the side nearest to the thumb.

- Helpful for sore throat, eyes, shoulder and neck problems and promotes feelings of calmness.

Large intestine 4 (LI4)

- Found on the back of the hand in the web between the thumb and index finger.

- Aids digestion and detoxification so helps improve the condition of the skin. Also relieves pain in the abdomen, constipation and headaches.

Small intestine 1 (SI1)

- Found on outside edge of the little finger by the corner of the fingernail.

- Helpful for stiff neck and headache.

Heart 7 (H7)

- Found on the outside edge of the first crease of the wrist closest to the palm, in the indent in line with the little finger.
- Improves circulation, calms the mind, relieves anxiety and insomnia.

Triple heater 4 (TH4)

- In the middle of the wrist joint on the back of the hand.
- Relieves pain in the wrists, hands and fingers.

CHAKRAS

Part of the traditional Indian belief is that the body contains chakras. As the foot is a map of the body, the chakras will also be found on the feet. The body has seven major chakras, which are all related to a colour:

- crown ⑦ which is violet
- brow (third eye) ⑥ which is dark blue
- throat ⑤ which is light blue
- heart ④ which is green
- solar plexus ③ which is yellow
- hara (or sacral) ② which is orange
- the base (or root) ①, which is red.

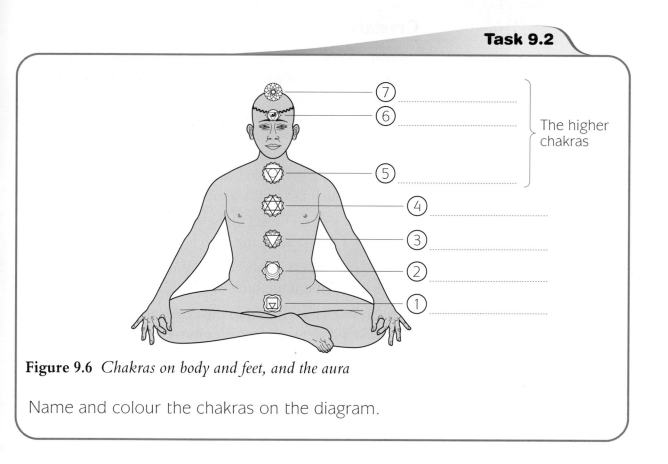

Figure 9.6 *Chakras on body and feet, and the aura*

Name and colour the chakras on the diagram.

The chakras are spinning circles of energy and are found about 3 cm (1 inch) away from the body. To ensure health the chakras need to unblocked, open and in balance with each other. Imbalances or blockages in the chakras can be helped by contact with an energy that nourishes or energy at a frequency that is beneficial to the chakras, such as the therapist's hands or crystals. Reflexology treatment will help to rebalance the chakras, which means they will be able to function properly so that they are not too open or too closed. When in a balanced state a person can remain calm in any situation. When out of balance, people tend to withdraw or feel overwhelmed or lose control of their emotions.

Crystals

Small, smooth crystals that are the same colours as the chakras may be used to help balance chakras. Place the stone onto the chakra area and exert pressure for a minute or two. You can use both hands to treat both feet at the same time. The following crystals may be used for each chakra:

- Crown chakra: found on top of the big toe. A violet stone such as amethyst can be placed here.

- Brow chakra: found in the upper region of the big toe. Use a dark-blue stone such as lapis lazuli.

- Throat chakra: found below the pad of the big toe. Use a light-blue stone such as turquoise.

- Heart chakra: found in the centre of the chest region. Use a green stone, such as moss agate. A pink stone such as rose quartz may also be used.

- Solar plexus chakra: found in the solar plexus reflex. Use a yellow or gold stone such as amber or tiger's eye.

- Sacral chakra: found on the area of the spine that represents the sacrum. Use an orange stone such as carnelian.

- Base chakra: found at the bottom of the spine area. Use a black stone such as haematite, or a red stone such as ruby.

Note

Coloured scarves may be used to help balance chakras.

AURAS

Energy from the universe, for example the sun and earth, passes through the chakras into the nadis, also known as meridians, that are invisible channels. The energy, prana, then passes into the body's cells. The nadis therefore connect the aura and chakras with the physical body. Energy that is not required by the body will leave the body through the chakras and the pores of the skin creating an aura also known as subtle bodies.

The aura is made up of levels of energy and in a healthy person forms an egg shape around the whole body. The more healthy an individual the further the aura will expand and the more colourful and vibrant it will be. It is said that great leaders from the past had auras that extended a vast distance, which may explain why they had so many followers. It is claimed that people who are happy and optimistic in life may live a lot longer than the miserable pessimistic types. Happy, healthy people will no doubt have vibrant, large auras, which may be why they are fun to be around and are generally popular. The aura can be weakened by poor diet, lack of exercise, stress, lack of rest, alcohol, drugs and tobacco.

Note

Animals and plants have auras too.

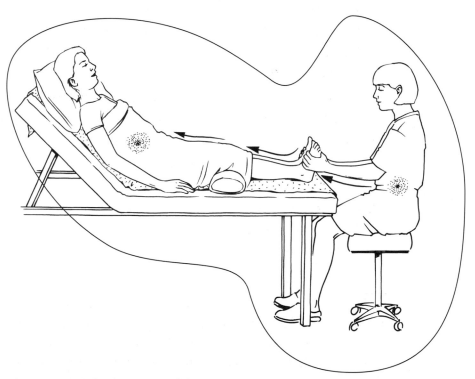

Figure 9.7 *The merging of the auras of the client and therapist during treatment*

Table 9.2

Therapy	Description
Acupressure	An ancient method of healing which uses the fingers and thumbs to apply pressure on the acupuncture points, lying along the meridians. Acupressure helps to promote a healthy flow of chi. It is useful in helping many conditions such as headache and nausea, and can be used on oneself
Acupuncture	There are about 2000 points along the meridians which are stimulated by the use of fine stainless steel needles. They are inserted through the skin to help balance the flow of the chi energy
Alexander technique	The Alexander technique involves correcting an individual's posture to help remove stress and tension from the body that may be the cause of illness and disease
Aromatherapy	The use of essential oils that have been extracted from various parts of plants. They can be used with carrier oils to either massage into the body, use in burners, or in the bath and compresses. The oil molecules enter the bloodstream and are taken around the body to help healing. The essential oils also have an effect on the limbic system, a part of the brain that deals with emotions. Care should be taken when using the oils as they are powerful substances
Bach flower remedies	Flower remedies are made from flowers and spring water and can affect the mood and alter our emotional state. Dr Bach's Rescue Remedy is a combination of five flower remedies and is useful to carry in case of emergencies such as shock
Bowen technique	A Bowen practitioner can feel whether muscles are stressed or tense and use gentle movements on the tissues to restore muscles to their normal state
Colour therapy	Colour has vibrational energy that can increase confidence and self-esteem. Colour and light can be used as healing tools, and crystals or coloured scarves can be used to help balance chakras
Chiropractic	Manipulation of the skeletal system, especially the spine. This releases joints and muscles that are stiff or painful in order to restore normal functioning

Table 9.2 (continued)

Therapy	Description
Crystal healing	Crystals and gems can be used to help promote emotional and physical healing. They may be carried, placed around the home or workplace, or placed around the body
Herbalism	Plants are used to aid healing and can help many conditions
Homeopathy	The theory of treating like with like forms the basis of homeopathy. To alleviate symptoms, e.g. sneezing, tiny amounts of a substance, e.g. cat fur, are chosen to help the body deal with the underlying causes and return the body back to a state of balance. There may be temporary worsening of symptoms before they disappear. The symptoms, personality type, build etc. are all taken into account when choosing a remedy to suit the individual
Iridology	The irises (the coloured part of the eye) can be studied to see if there are any physical or emotional problems in the body
Kinesiology	This treatment involves muscle testing by placing the limbs in different positions and then applying pressure to them. The therapist can determine if there are energy blockages in the body
Massage	Manipulation of the muscles using the hands to help release tension
Nutritional therapy	Advice regarding diet is given to help cleanse and heal the body
Osteopathy	Problems with the musculoskeletal system are diagnosed and corrected. Postural advice is given as pain, stiffness, immobility and deformity can result from bad postural habits, old injuries or stress
Physiotherapy	Massage and physical exercise are used to relieve pain and muscular tension. It is often used to help people after an accident, illness or major surgery
Reiki	The Reiki healer uses their hands to aid the flow of energy in the body. By using the hands in certain positions on the body the healer can help to release emotional and physical blockages and promote relaxation and healing
Shiatsu	Therapy that uses the hands and combines massage, acupressure and some manipulation. It helps to improve circulation, detoxify and stimulate the body's healing energy

Table 9.2 (continued)

Therapy	Description
Thermal auricular therapy	This therapy involves using tubes impregnated with herbs, and these are lit and placed in the ear. The candle burns down and helps to soften and loosen ear wax and promote relaxation as well as helping many other conditions
Yoga	An ancient practice involving the mind, body and spirit, which uses exercises and focuses on breathing and meditation. Different postures are performed to stretch the muscles and help stimulate the release of endorphins, which lift the mood and give a sense of well-being. Yoga helps to increase flexibility and strength

Legislation, good practice and setting up a business 10

It is important to understand the health, safety and hygiene regulations relating to reflexology treatment. Reflexologists need to be aware of the following legislation and guidelines.

LEGISLATION FOR THE REFLEXOLOGIST

Health and Safety at Work Act 1974

This Act is aimed at ensuring that employers and employees maintain high standards of health and safety in the workplace.

Employers are responsible for the health and safety of everyone who enters their premises. If an employer has more than five employees, the workplace must have a health and safety policy which all staff must be aware of.

Employers and employees have responsibilities under this Act. Employers must ensure the following:

- that the workplace does not pose a risk to the health and safety of employees and clients
- that protective equipment is provided
- all equipment must be safe and have regular checks
- there must be a safe system of cash handling, such as when taking money to the bank
- staff should be aware of safety procedures in the workplace, and have the necessary information, instruction and training.

Employees' responsibilities include:

◆ following the health and safety policy

◆ reading the hazard warning labels on containers and following the advice

◆ reporting any potential hazard (such as glass breakage, spillage of chemicals etc.) to the relevant person in the workplace.

The Health and Safety (First Aid) Regulations 1981

A place of work must have a first-aid box containing the following: plasters, bandages, wound dressings, safety pins, eyepads and cleaning wipes.

When first aid is given, relevant information must be recorded such as the patient's name, the date, place, time, events, the injury and treatment/advice given.

Basic first aid in the workplace

Table 10.1 Basic first aid

Problem	First-aid procedure
Allergies	If the skin is red, itchy and inflamed after using oil or cream the client may have an allergy. Firstly remove the product using water. If possible apply a cold compress or cold pack to reduce the swelling
Burns	The affected area should be held under cold running water for a few minutes. If the burn is serious, medical attention should be sought; however, it can be covered loosely with a sterile dressing in the meantime
Cuts	Remember to put on disposable gloves as soon as possible. Rinse the cut under running water. If there is bleeding, sterile gauze or a pad of cotton wool can be placed over the wound. Keep the affected part elevated if possible and apply pressure for a few minutes. Seek medical attention if the bleeding does not stop

Table 10.1 (continued)

Problem	First-aid procedure
Dizziness	The client should be positioned with their head down between their knees. This will help blood to flow to the head
Electric shock	The person must not be touched until disconnected from the electricity supply. A qualified person can give artificial respiration. Call for an ambulance
Epilepsy	If a person is having an epileptic fit, remove any items around them that could cause injury.
Fainting	Lay the person flat and place pillows under the lower legs. This will increase the flow of blood to the head
Fall	Do not move the person if they complain of back or neck pain. Cover them with a blanket and call an ambulance
Nose bleeds	Sit the client in a chair with their head bent forward. Ask them to firmly pinch the soft part of the nose until bleeding stops
Objects in the eye	Twist a dampened piece of cotton wool or tissue and try to move the object to the inside corner of the eye. Otherwise, wash the object out using eye solution in an eye bath

Fire Precautions Act 1971

This Act states that all staff must be trained in fire and emergency evacuation procedure and the premises must have fire escapes.

- There must be adequate fire-fighting equipment in good working order.

- Clearly marked fire exit doors should remain unlocked and must not be obstructed.

- Smoke alarms must be used.

- All staff must be trained in fire drill procedures and this information should be displayed at the workplace.

Fire extinguishers

Fire extinguishers are colour coded for different types of fire. Table 10.2 states the colour, contents and type of fire extinguisher to be used in different situations.

Table 10.2 Fire extinguishers

Colour	Contents of fire extinguisher	Type of fire it is used for
Red (water)	Water	Wood, paper, clothing and plastics
Blue (dry powder)	Dry powder	Electrical fires, oils, alcohols, solvents, paint. Flammable liquids and gases. (Not on chip- or fat-pan fires)
Cream (foam)	Foam	Flammable liquids. Do not use on electrical fires
Black (CO_2)	Carbon dioxide (CO_2)	For use on electrical fires but switch off electricity supply first. Grease, fats, oil, paint, flammable liquids. (Not on chip- or fat-pan fires)

Fire blankets are used to put out fires such as chip-pan fires. The blanket covers the fire and helps prevent oxygen from fuelling the flames and so the fire is extinguished.

Control of Substances Hazardous to Health (COSHH) 1994

COSHH covers substances used in practice which can cause ill health. Hazardous substances such as oils must be used and stored away safely. All containers that contain potentially harmful chemicals must be labelled clearly. Manufacturers often give safety information regarding their products.

Corrosive

Oxidising

Toxic

Harmful irritant

Highly flammable

Explosive

Figure 10.1 *Hazard symbols*

Environmental Protection Act 1990

This Act is concerned with the disposal of waste. Any waste should be disposed of safely and the manufacturer's instructions should be followed.

Electricity at Work Act 1989

This Act is concerned with safety while using electricity. All electrical equipment must be checked regularly to ensure it is safe. All checks should be listed in a record book, and that book would be important evidence if there was any legal action.

Reporting of Injuries, Diseases and Dangerous Occurrences Regulations (RIDDOR) 1995

Minor accidents should be entered into a record book, stating what occurred and what action was taken. Ideally all concerned should sign. The employer should send a report to the local authority environmental health department as soon as possible if, as a result of an accident at work, anyone:

- is off work for more than three days
- is seriously injured
- has a type of occupational disease certified by the doctor
- dies.

Manual Handling Operations Regulations 1992

Incorrect lifting and carrying of goods can result in injuries such as back injury. Employers must assess the risks to their employees and make sure they provide training if necessary.

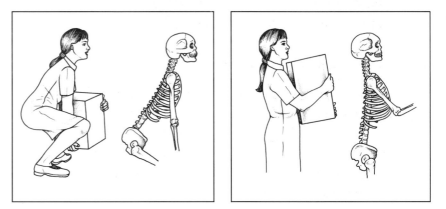

Figure 10.2 *To avoid injury when lifting, keep your knees bent and your back straight at all times*

Local Government Act 1982

Byelaws are laws made by local councils and are primarily concerned with hygiene practice. Different councils around the country will have different byelaws. You will probably find there is not a byelaw relating to reflexology treatment in your area. However, advice can be sought from the local environmental health officer. A therapist must apply for a licence from the local Environmental Health and Trading Standards Department if needles are used for any treatments such as acupuncture or ear and body piercing.

Performing Rights

Some therapists like to play relaxing music whilst giving a treatment. Any music played in waiting or treatment rooms is considered a public performance. If you play music you may need to purchase a licence from Phonographic Performance Ltd (PPL) or from the Performing Rights Society (PRS). These organisations collect the licence fees and pay the performer and record companies. If you do not buy a licence, legal action may be taken against you.

However, many composers of music are not members of the PPL or PRS so no fee will need to be paid. To find out if you need a licence contact the supplier of the music.

Data Protection Act 1998

Any business that stores information about individuals (e.g. clients) on a computer must be registered with the data protection register. The Act aims to ensure that this information is used by authorised individuals only (e.g. the therapist) and is not given to anyone else without the client's permission. As yet this Act does not apply to records stored manually, such as record cards stored in boxes.

The Consumer Protection Act 1987

This Act provides the customer with protection when purchasing goods or services to ensure that products are safe for use on the client during the treatment, or are safe to be sold as a retail product.

In the past if a person was injured they had to prove that the manufacturer was negligent before they could sue for damages. This Act removed the need to prove negligence. A customer can sue a supplier without having to prove they were negligent.

Cosmetic Products (Safety) Regulations 1996

These relate to the Consumer Protection Act 1987 and require that cosmetics and toiletries are tested and safe for use.

Trade Descriptions Acts 1968 and 1972

A description of a product or service, either spoken or written, must be accurate. It is illegal to use false or misleading descriptions to sell, e.g. stating a product can cure a skin disorder if that information is inaccurate.

The Sale and Supply of Goods Act 1994 (replaced the Sales of Goods and Services Act 1982)

This Act identifies the contract, which results between the seller (therapist) and the customer (client) when a product is purchased. The Act makes the seller responsible for ensuring that the goods are of good merchantable quality. It covers all goods, even those used as part of the treatment. It requires that the person giving the service must act with reasonable care and skill, within a reasonable time and for a reasonable charge.

Prohibited Appellation

It is a criminal offence for anyone who does not hold the appropriate qualifications to state that they have occupations that include the following: doctor, dentist, chemist, chiropodist, veterinary surgeon, midwife and nurse.

The Sex Discrimination Acts 1975 and 1986 and the Race Relations Act 1976

The Equal Opportunities Commission investigates complaints alleging discrimination against job applicants because of their sex, race or marital status.

Note

Under the Trade Descriptions Acts 1968 and 1972, a product should be sold at its full price for at least 28 days before it can be offered at a reduced price.

Protection of Children Act 1999

Employers involved in the care of children (i.e. anyone under 18 years old), can check the names of people they intend to employ to ensure they are not included in a list called the Consultancy Index List. This list contains names of individuals considered unsuitable to work with children.

Disability Discrimination Act 1995 (DDA 1995)

Businesses providing a service to the public need to ensure that they make their services available and accessible to disabled customers. This Act states that reasonable adjustments should be made to features such as steps, stairways, entrances and wash rooms.

CODES OF PRACTICE AND CODES OF ETHICS

Industry Codes of Practice for Hygiene in Salons and Clinics

Professional reflexology associations will have a code of practice which is concerned with hygiene in the salon and gives guidelines for the therapist. Local byelaws also contain these guidelines to ensure good hygiene practice and to avoid cross-infection.

Industry Code of Ethics

A professional massage therapist must ensure the following:

- All health, safety and hygiene legislation is adhered to and the therapist is adequately insured.
- The best possible treatment is given to the client.
- The client is respected and dignity is maintained at all times.
- They never claim to cure a condition.
- They do not treat a client who is contraindicated to treatment.

- All clients are treated in a professional manner regardless of their colour, sex or religion.

- All information given, written or verbal, is confidential and should not be disclosed to anyone without written permission except when required to do so by law.

- Records of treatments carried out are up to date and complete.

- Further training is undertaken to enhance skills.

- They become a member of a professional reflexology association.

INSURANCE

Employers Liability Act 1969

Employers must take out insurance policies in case of claims by employees for injury, disease or illness related to the workplace. It protects an employer in the event of claims made by an employee. A certificate must be displayed at work to show that the employer has this insurance.

Public liability insurance

This insurance protects you if a client or member of the public is injured on your premises.

Product liability insurance

This type of insurance protects you against claims arising from products used by clients.

Treatment liability insurance

This insurance covers the reflexologist for damage to clients caused by the treatment itself.

Complete the table to give a brief description of the legislation and insurance.

Table 10.3 Legislation

Legislation/guidelines	Brief description
Health and Safety at Work Act 1974	
Health and Safety (First Aid) Regulations 1981	
Fire Precautions Act 1971	
COSHH 1994	
Environmental Protection Act 1990	
Electricity at Work Act 1989	
RIDDOR 1995	
Manual Handling Operations Regulations 1992	
Local Government Act 1982	
Performing Rights	
Data Protection Act 1998	

Table 10.3 (Continued)

Consumer Protection Act 1987	
Cosmetic Products (Safety) Regulations 1996	
Trade Descriptions Acts 1968 and 1972	
The Sale and Supply of Goods Act 1994	
Prohibited Appellation	
Sex Discrimination Acts 1975 and 1986 and the Race Relations Act 1976	
Protection of Children Act 1999	
Disability Discrimination Act 1995	
Employers Liability Act 1969	
Public liability insurance	
Product liability insurance	
Treatment liability insurance	

STARTING A REFLEXOLOGY BUSINESS

If you intend to set up a business the following information will help you to prepare your business plan.

Note

Banks will give you professional advice regarding setting up a business.

Research plan

♦ Research local competition. How much do they charge for treatments? What are their hours of business?

♦ Research the price of products and equipment that you will need to start your business.

♦ How will you advertise and maintain public relations? How much will advertising your business cost?

♦ Carry out market research in the area where you propose to run your business. Are people interested in the services you have to offer?

♦ Will you be self financed or will you require external finance, such as a loan? Consider seeking the professional advice of an accountant.

♦ What insurance policies will you need to take out and how much will they cost?

♦ Will you rent a room and, if so, how much will you pay?

♦ Will you run a mobile business? What costs are involved?

♦ Research all health, safety and hygiene issues and cost these in if necessary.

♦ Consider the catchment area; who are you trying to attract and from where?

♦ If you take over an existing business, what improvements could you make?

Treatment room

♦ What are the considerations when choosing the location of a treatment room, e.g. is there room for clients to park nearby, or will there be passing trade?

♦ What colour scheme will you have for your room?

♦ Draw a plan of your treatment room and consider all of the equipment and resources you will need.

Note

It is a good idea to design a price list, and any other leaflet, which gives a brief outline of the services you will provide.

Clients and services

◆ How will you ensure client satisfaction so that the client returns for future treatments?

◆ How much will you charge clients for each treatment? How long will each treatment take? You will need to ensure the treatments are cost effective.

◆ How will you advertise your business?

◆ How will you ensure that you maximise profitability, e.g. timekeeping, minimum wastage etc.?

◆ Will you require staff?

Business plan

Producing a business plan is similar to planning an event such as a wedding. To ensure everything runs smoothly all factors should be considered and planned, and costs should be taken into account if there is a budget. A business plan will help you to think about all aspects of your business to help ensure success and business growth. If you are setting up a business the following website will be useful, www.businesslink.gov.uk.

Example of a business plan

BUSINESS DETAILS

Name of business
Address of business

Status of business
Type of business
Telephone
Date business began (if you have already started trading)
Business activities

PERSONAL DETAILS

Name
Address

Telephone (home)   Telephone (work)
Qualifications

                                                   Date of birth

Relevant work experience

Business experience

Details of personnel (if any)
Name   Name
Position   Position
Address   Address

Date of birth   Date of birth
Qualifications   Qualifications

Relevant work experience   Relevant work experience

Present income   Present income
What skills will you need to buy in during the first two years?

PERSONNEL

Estimate the cost of employing any people or buying any services you may need in the first two years?

Number of people	Job function	Monthly cost	Annual cost

(Remember to include you own salary and those of any you may have in this calculation.)

continued

Figure 10.3 *Business plan*
Adapted from Mernagh-Ward D. and Cartwright J. (1997) *Good Practice in Salon Management*, Nelson Thornes Ltd

PRODUCT SERVICE
Description of type of products/services to be offered.

Contribution of individual products or services to total turnover
Product   Percentage contribution

                                                                           (The figures in this column should add up to 100.)

Break down the cost of materials (if any)
PRODUCT I
Materials (including packaging, labelling etc.)   Cost

*Selling price for Product I
PRODUCT 2

*Selling price for Product 2
PRODUCT 3

*Selling price for Product 3
(*These are assumptions)
Where did you get your estimate from?
Material   Source

MARKET
Describe your market

Where is you market?

Who are your customers?

Is you market growing, static or in decline?

Itemise the competitive products or services
Name of competitor I
Competitor's product/service
Name   Price
Strengths   Weakness

Name of competitor 2
Competitor's product/service
Name   Price
Strengths   Weakness

Name of competitor 3
Competitor's product/service
Name   Price
Strengths   Weakness

continued

Figure 10.3 *Business plan (continued)*

What is special about your product or service?

Advantages of your product or service over competitor 1

Competitor 2

Competitor 3

What is your sales forecast for the
*1st three months? Total value
Treatments/products
*2nd three months? Total value
Treatments/products
*3rd three months? Total value
Treatments/products
*4th three months Total value
Treatments/products
(*These are assumptions)

Explain how you have calculated these estimates

Give details of any firm orders you have already taken

MARKETING

What sort of marketing do your competitors do?
Competitor 1

Competitor 2

Competitor 3

What sort of marketing or advertising do you intend to do?
Method Cost

Why do you, think that these methods are appropriate for your particular market?

Where did you get your estimates from?
Method Source

PREMISES/EQUIPMENT/PRODUCT
PREMISES:
Where do you intend to locate the business and why?

What sort and size of premises will you need?

What are the details of any lease, licence, rent, rates and when is the next rent review due?

continued

Figure 10.3 *Business plan (continued)*

What equipment and products do you require?

Is equipment bought or leased and how long is the life span?

On what terms will the products be purchased?

RECORDS
Describe records to be kept and how they are to be kept up to date?

OBJECTIVES
What are your personal objectives in running the business?
Short-term

Medium-term

Long-term

How do you intend to achieve them?

What objectives do you have for the business itself?
Short-term

Medium-term

Long-term

How do you intend to achieve them?

FINANCE
Give details of your known orders and sales (if any)

	Date	Orders/sales	Details	Delivery date
1				
2				
3				
4				

Give details of your current business assets (if any)

Item	Value	Life expectancy

continued

Figure 10.3 *Business plan (continued)*

What will you need to buy to start up and then throughout your first year?

Start up

Item	Value

Year I

Item	Value

How will you pay for these?	Value	Date
Grants		
Own resources		
Loans		
Creditors		

What credit is available from your suppliers?

Supplier	Estimated value of monthly order	Number of days credit

What are your loan or overdraft requirements?

What are you putting in yourself?

What security will you be able to put up?

OTHER

Accountant
Address

Telephone

Solicitor
Address

Telephone

VAT registration
Insurance arrangements

Figure 10.3 *Business plan (continued)*

Examination preparation

These multiple-choice questions will help you to prepare for reflexology examinations. Decide which is the correct answer and put a circle around either a, b, c or d.

1 Who discovered the zones of the body and called the technique zone therapy?

  a Joe Riley
  b William Fitzgerald
  c Eunice Ingham
  d Edwin Bowers.

2 Who discovered that using pressure techniques on the soles of the feet could heal parts of the body and also made a detailed chart of the reflexes?

  a Charles Sherrington
  b Sir Henry Head
  c Eunice Ingham
  d William Fitzgerald.

3 Integral biology is the study of the:

  a endocrine system
  b effect of the environment on our physical and mental health
  c bones of the feet
  d effects of stress on our feet.

4 Which of the following is a contraindication to reflexology treatment?

    a Diabetes
    b Vitiligo
    c Irritable bowel syndrome
    d Headaches.

5 The outer side of the foot is known as the:

    a medial surface
    b plantar surface
    c dorsal surface
    d lateral surface.

6 The cross-referral area of the knee is the:

    a hip
    b elbow
    c ankle
    d shoulder.

7 Which of the following is *not* a bone of the foot?

    a Calcaneus
    b Navicular
    c Hamate
    d Talus.

8 Which of the following is a bone found in the hand?

    a Humerus
    b Metatarsal
    c Radius
    d Scaphoid.

9 Which of the following is *not* a muscle found in the lower leg and foot?

    a Gastrocnemius muscle
    b Flexor digitorum brevis
    c Thenar muscles
    d Abductor hallucis.

10 Which of the following is *not* a condition found in the foot?

    a Sinusitis
    b Athlete's foot
    c Bunion
    d Gout.

11 Zone 1 runs through:

    a the centre of the body
    b the eye to the second finger and third toe
    c the ear to the little finger and fifth toe
    d the ear and to the third finger and fourth toe.

12 The liver reflex can be found:

    a above the diaphragm line
    b below the diaphragm line
    c on the toes
    d below the waistline.

13 Which of the following structures does *not* make up the large intestine?

    a Sigmoid flexure
    b Hepatic flexure
    c Transverse colon
    d Duodenum.

14 The fallopian tube reflexes can be found on the:

    a lateral surface of the foot
    b dorsal surface of the foot
    c medial surface of the foot
    d plantar surface of the foot.

15 The heart reflex can be found:

    a on the client's left foot above the diaphragm line
    b on the client's right foot below the waistline
    c on the dorsal aspect of the foot above the diaphragm line
    d on the lateral side of the foot above the waistline.

16 The spine is found on the:

   a lateral side of the foot
   b medial side of the foot
   c on the plantar surface of the foot
   d on the dorsal surface of the foot.

17 Which of the following is *not* a reflexology technique used when carrying out treatment?

   a Hook in, back up
   b Rotations
   c Hacking
   d Thumb/finger walk.

18 Which of the following is *not* a healing crisis that may happen after treatment is given?

   a Nausea
   b Headache
   c Bleeding
   d Tiredness.

19 Which two reflexes are found in the big toe?

   a Pituitary/kidney
   b Thyroid/hypothalamus
   c Pineal/pituitary
   d Heart/hypothalamus.

20 Reflex areas for the sinuses are found:

   a in the tip of the big toe only
   b in the tips of the toes
   c in the balls of the feet
   d below the diaphragm under the fourth toe.

21 An ingrowing toenail could relate to:

   a ear ache
   b headaches/migraines
   c chest pain
   d toothache.

22 A high or fallen arch may be directly related to:

    a back or spinal problems
    b reproductive problems
    c headaches/migraines
    d fluid retention.

23 The direct reflex area to treat for irritable bowel syndrome would be:

    a large intestine
    b liver
    c bladder
    d gall bladder.

24 The direct reflexes for emphysema are:

    a sinuses, lungs
    b lungs, bronchi
    c bronchi, head
    d bronchi, sinuses.

25 Working the duodenal reflex helps to:

    a encourage sweat excretion
    b improve lymphatic drainage
    c improve circulation
    d improve digestion.

26 The uterus reflexes are found on the:

    a dorsal surface of the foot
    b plantar surface of the foot
    c lateral side of the foot
    d the medial side of the foot.

27 The pituitary gland is found:

    a on the big toes
    b on the little toes
    c on the heel of the foot
    d between the toes.

28 When would the hand be worked instead of the foot?

   a When treatment on the feet is contraindicated
   b When treating young children
   c When treating headaches
   d When the client is stressed.

29 Oestopathy is defined as diagnosis and treatment of mechanical problems in the:

   a musculoskeletal system
   b circulatory systems
   c muscular system
   d spine.

30 Crystals in relation to reflexology treatment are thought to be:

   a uric acid crystals that build up on the end of nerve endings
   b stones used to enhance healing effects
   c hardened areas of scar tissue
   d a sign of good muscle tone.

31 Many sensations felt in the foot, such as grittiness and hardness, can indicate poor energy flow in the body. Which of the following would a therapist *not* do to help treat this imbalance?

   a Work slower and deeper over the affected area
   b Press and rotate over the area for a longer time
   c Work over the area many times
   d Ignore this area and work it on the following treatment.

32 The stomach meridian can be found ending on the top of the:

   a big toe
   b second toe
   c fourth toe
   d little toe.

33 The function of the ileo-caecal valve is to:

    a help the body to absorb nutrients
    b prevent the waste matter going back into the small intestine
    c help the absorption of fats
    d store waste until it leaves the anus.

34 The sciatic nerve can be found:

    a across the heel and up the back of the foot
    b across the waistline and up the back of the foot
    c running along zone 2
    d in zone 5.

35 Elimination of toxins is important to the health of the body. Which of the following is *not* an eliminatory channel?

    a Large intestine
    b Skin
    c Lungs
    d Ears.

36 Which of the following would be aftercare advice given after reflexology treatment?

    a Consume lots of drinks containing caffeine
    b Drink plenty of water to flush out toxins
    c Do some vigorous exercise
    d Eat a three-course meal.

37 If a client fainted what course of action would be taken?

    a Lay the person flat and place pillows under the lower legs
    b Try to stand them up
    c Offer a glass of water
    d Sit them on a chair.

38 The initials COSHH stand for:

   a control of substances hurtful to health
   b control of substances hazardous to health
   c control of situation hazardous to health
   d control of substances helpful to health.

39 Which of the following types of legislation relates directly to employers and employees maintaining high standards of health and safety?

   a Consumer Protection Act 1987
   b RIDDOR 1995
   c Data Protection Act 1998
   d Health and Safety at Work Act 1974.

40 Prohibited appellation means that:

   a the therapist is not allowed to swear
   b it is an offence to state you have a certain occupation without holding relevant qualifications
   c it is an offence to discriminate against someone because of their sex, race or marital status
   d it is illegal to treat a child.

Index